FRUIT FANDANGO

FRUIT
FANDANGO

MOYA CLARKE

CHARTWELL
BOOKS, INC.

A QUINTET BOOK

Published by Chartwell Books
A Division of Book Sales, Inc.
110 Enterprise Avenue
Secaucus, New Jersey 07094

This edition produced for sale
in the U.S.A., its territories
and dependencies only.

ISBN 0-7858-0091-3

This book was designed and produced by
Quintet Publishing Limited
6 Blundell Street
London N7 9BH

Creative Director: Richard Dewing
Designer: Suzie Hooper
Project Editor: Stefanie Foster
Copy Editor: Diana Vowles
Home Economist: Nicole Szabason
Photographer: Nick Bailey
Photographic Assistants: Chris Brown,
Jenny Wells
Illustrator: Jake Rickwood

Typeset in Great Britain by
Central Southern Typesetters, Eastbourne
Manufactured in Singapore by
Bright Arts Pte. Ltd
Printed in Singapore by
Star Standard Industries Pte. Ltd

CONTENTS

WIZARD WAYS WITH FRUIT

FRUIT IS NO longer a seasonal food – it is now transported across continents so that we can all take full advantage of a multi-national harvest throughout the year. This book presents a collection of recipes to inspire every cook to create dishes

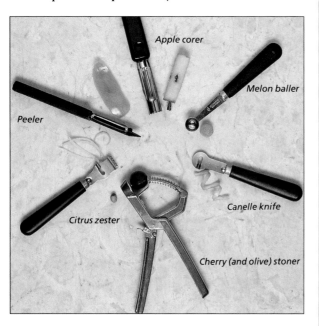

both savory and sweet, both quick to prepare for light meals and fabulous for more formal dinner parties.

Exotic fruit really allow for imaginative and exciting cooking which reflects the color and warmth of their countries of origin. As well as browsing the displays in larger supermarkets, visit street markets and ethnic stores which often have the most unusual produce on offer. Buy from stores and markets which obviously have a high turnover in order to be sure of finding good quality and do not be tempted to buy large quantities which you are unable to use quickly – unless, of course, you are having a preserving session.

Take care over the choice of fruit for a menu – think about the balance of the meal and the tastes of guests. Don't plan something exotic unless you will be serving the dish to those with a cosmopolitan approach to food – the traditional "meat-and-two-veg" person may not appreciate a fruit-laden main dish.

Even though simple fruits are on offer all year, it is still best to make the most of locally grown prod-

uce in season; sun-ripened on the plant and hand-picked by yourself shortly before you cook, it will have the finest flavor. With so many fruit farms offering picking facilities, you should be able to find one within a reasonable distance. Pick only as much as you can use or freeze and be prepared to process all the fruit into the freezer promptly when you get home.

A great bowl of fruit looks wonderful as a dinner-table centerpiece but this is not the best way to store fruit. If the fruit needs to be ripened for eating it should be stored at room temperature, but not highly stacked where pieces underneath may be bruised. Soft fruit is often best refrigerated, especially in hot weather, and other fruits should be kept in a cool room away from direct sunlight.

The remainder of this opening chapter offers general advice on dealing with different fruit, while the recipes include appropriate preparation instructions and cooking methods. The glossary at the end of the book offers guidance on using a broad range of exotic fruit, along with ideas for a more familiar harvest. I hope you will discover something new and enjoy experimenting with less familiar ingredients as much as I have enjoyed creating and sampling the recipes.

CHOICE, STORAGE, AND PREPARATION

The following information outlines key points to remember when buying and using different groups of fruit. An A–Z listing of individual types of fruit may be found in the glossary on page 118.

APPLES AND PEARS

These are versatile fruits for eating fresh and for cooking. There is a wide choice of varieties available, with markedly different flavors and textures.

When buying apples, select firm, unblemished fruit with fresh-looking, bright skin. Avoid those that are slightly wrinkled or soft.

Pears vary according to type: ripe, juicy pears for eating should feel plump and tender. If they are soft or slightly squashy, they may be overripe. When selecting pears for cooking, look for firm fruit which will peel well and retain its shape during cooking.

In the short term, apples and pears should be kept in a cool place, not too highly stacked or the

6

fruit underneath will be bruised. Do not refrigerate the fruit and do not keep it in a warm room for long as it will lose moisture and become soft, tough-skinned, and slightly wrinkled.

Apples may be stored for long periods if they are perfect when picked. Do not attempt to store any fruit with blemished skin as these small patches rot. The fruit should be picked when dry and layered between paper or cardboard in a cardboard box. The apples must not touch each other – wrapping each apple in paper is the best method of protecting the fruit, and this also prevents any rot which may develop in one apple from spreading to other fruit. The apples should be kept in a cool, dark place, preferably with a tendency towards dampness – a cellar or shed is ideal provided it is free of vermin. In this way, some types of fruit will keep for several months or throughout the winter. If you want to buy a box of apples to keep, ask the grocer's advice first – most reputable traders will suggest the best variety and advise on whether the fruit is in ideal condition for keeping.

PREPARATION

Apples and pears may be used with or without the peel on, depending on the recipe. Some apples cook and look better with the peel on. Once peeled, the fruit will discolor and some varieties rapidly turn brown. To prevent this, the fruit may be placed in water with a little lemon juice, vinegar or salt added as soon as it is peeled, and kept submerged until it is used.

Coring whole fruit Use an apple corer to remove the central core from whole apples, for example before baking. Stand the apple on a board and push the corer firmly down through the middle of the fruit, then remove it to bring out a column of core. Since the majority of apples do not have perfectly central cores, you usually have to turn the apple upside down and repeat the coring at a slightly different angle to remove the remaining core.

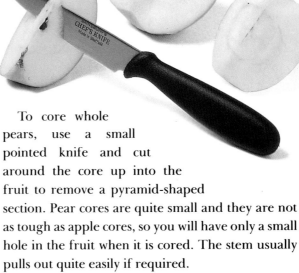

To core whole pears, use a small pointed knife and cut around the core up into the fruit to remove a pyramid-shaped section. Pear cores are quite small and they are not as tough as apple cores, so you will have only a small hole in the fruit when it is cored. The stem usually pulls out quite easily if required.

Peeling and coring A common method of preparing apples is to cut each fruit into four, then to cut out the section of core before thinly peeling the fruit. This gives neatly peeled and cored apple quarters, ready for poaching or for slicing and using in pies, flans, tarts, and sauces, or for cooking to a purée.

Alternatively, thinly remove the peel from the cored whole apple, working around the fruit, then slice the apple into rings.

To peel whole pears, use a vegetable peeler or small fine knife and work down the fruit, from stem to core, in even strips. It is easier to remove the core before peeling whole pears.

LARGE FRUIT WITH PITS: PEACHES, NECTARINES, APRICOTS, AND PLUMS

Varieties of fruit with pits are available in most months, although the price fluctuates according to availability. (See glossary, page 118, for examples of specific varieties.) You can obtain fruit with pits frozen in syrup, but it tends to collapse; however, frozen plums are useful for baked desserts and for purées. The more space-saving method of freezing is to purée the fruit first, adding a little lemon juice to peaches and nectarines to prevent discoloration. The thawed purées may be used for sauces, soufflés, mousses, and other sweet dishes. Generally, fruit for savory dishes is used in pieces, such as halves or slices. The tangy flavor of this fruit is particularly complementary to rich meats and poultry, such as ham, pork, lamb, or duck.

7

Look for fruit which is firm but not hard. Over-ripe fruit has less flavor and the pleasant tang associated with plums is lost; apricots tend to be woolly. Fruit which is overripe is best puréed.

Cut peaches, nectarines, and apricots discolor on exposure to air, so they should be sprinkled with a little lemon juice as soon as they are prepared unless they are to be used immediately.

Halving and pitting Some varieties are easiest to stone, since the pit sits loosely in its cavity. The method for all fruit with large pits is the same: cut around the fruit down to the pit. Holding one half

of the fruit in the palm of one hand, gently twist the other half to free the pit. Separate the fruit and carefully cut the pit from the half in which it remains.

Peeling Peaches and nectarines are usually peeled; you can peel apricots if the recipe specifies this or if you don't like the slightly furry skin. Plums are not peeled.

Place the fruit in a bowl and pour in freshly boiling water to cover it. Leave to stand for 20–40 seconds. The time depends on the ripeness of the fruit – the firmer it is the longer the time required to free the skin. Drain the fruit and immerse it in iced water to prevent further softening. Use a sharp pointed knife to slit the skin from the stem end; if it has been blanched sufficiently, the skin will peel off easily.

Slicing Peaches and nectarines may need to be sliced for a recipe. You can pit and halve the fruit first, then slice it; alternatively, it is usually possible to cut the fruit off the pit in wedges. Cut from stem end to base down to the pit, then make a second cut at an

angle into the same place and twist the cut wedge free of the pit. Cut away further slices, working around one side, then start again from the original cut edge and cut off the remaining fruit. The slices are not as even as when cut from halved and pitted fruit but this is a quick method.

CHERRIES

Cherry varieties may be loosely divided into sweet and bitter, the latter being used for cooking rather than for eating raw. Look for firm, shiny fruit which is not bruised or damaged. Reject fruit which has been pecked by birds.

Cherries have a wide variety of uses in sweet and savory dishes such as salads, pies, flans, and preserves. Bitter cherries are used in a classic sauce for duck, and they also go well with rich meats or poultry. Firm cherries freeze well, either plain or in a syrup. Always pit fruit before freezing as the task is extremely difficult when the fruit softens on thawing.

Pitting A cherry pitter is essential if the fruit is to be left whole. This small two-armed gadget consists of a cherry-sized cup with a pit-sized hole in its base at the end of one arm and a prong on the end of the other arm. Remove the stem from a cherry and place it in the cup, with the stem end up. Hold the pitter over a bowl and close the pronged arm: the prong pierces the cherry and pushes out the pit.

If you do not have a pitter, use a small sharp knife to slit a cherry down one side, then prise out the pit. This is a tedious operation when preparing more than a few cherries and the fruit tends to be squashed and broken.

SOFT FRUIT: BERRIES

This category includes currants, gooseberries, strawberries, raspberries, mulberries, blueberries, bilberries, loganberries and so on, all of which are listed in the glossary on page 118. Generally, all soft fruits freeze well but some collapse badly when thawed, notably strawberries and gooseberries. These are best puréed before freezing.

Look for fruit which is ripe but firm – overripe fruit will have less flavor and may even taste musty or slightly unpleasant. Inspect cartons of bought fruit carefully for any signs of mold as this will taint the surrounding berries. Discard any damaged or moldy fruit.

Pick fruit such as strawberries, raspberries, and blackberries on a dry day and as early in the day as possible. After long periods of drought the fruit will be inferior unless it has been watered regularly. Do not pick immediately after very wet weather as the fruit tends to be damaged and may become moldy more quickly. Raspberries and mulberries should be picked off their stems, leaving their centers hollow.

PREPARATION

Rinse the fruit in small batches in a colander under cold running water. Do not leave to soak. Wild blackberries are an exception as these should be washed in a bowl of water with a little salt added to draw out insects and any maggots which may be present.

Hulling This is the term for removing stems from strawberries. Hold the calyx (the green top) firmly and twist it gently as you pull it out of the fruit. The white hull or core will come out in one piece attached to the calyx.

Trimming This is the method of preparing gooseberries. Pinch off both ends of each fruit, removing the stem and the slightly spiky, brown base. This is a slow task, best tackled sitting down, but it is essential if cooked dishes are not to be spoilt by the unpleasant prickly bits at either end of the fruit. This is not necessary if the fruit is to be cooked, puréed and sieved.

Stringing Currants (black, red, and white) are removed from their stems by stringing. The currants are picked by snipping off small bunches of fruit. Hold the end of the bunch, dangling the fruit over a basin, and use a fork to scrape the fruit off the stems. Pick stems off individual currants by hand.

9

GRAPES

Green, black, and red grapes, seedless or with seeds, are commonly available. Buy plump, undamaged fruit which is not squashed or tightly packed in displays. Look for nicely shaped bunches if you intend displaying them on a cheeseboard or in an arrangement of fruit. Keep the grapes in a cool place.

PREPARATION

Wash the bunches of grapes under cold running water and pat them dry on paper towels or a clean cloth. Do not place them in a dish until all the water has dripped off.

Peeling This is a tedious job. Use a small sharp knife and carefully peel off the skin in strips from the top to the bottom of each grape.

Seeding Cut each grape in half and use the point of a knife to pick out the seeds.

MELONS

These are wonderful fruit, available in one form or another all year. Choose large, heavy melons which have firm skin; avoid those that look dull or slightly wrinkled. Press the stem end – the circular area around the top of the melon will give very slightly if it is ripe. Avoid fruit with any soft or dark patches or signs of mold.

PREPARATION

Removing seeds Halve the melon and scoop out the seeds with a spoon. Discard any slightly woolly, stringy flesh immediately below the seeds – this usually comes out easily as the seeds are scraped away.

Watermelon has shiny black seeds dotted through the flesh. Cut watermelon into wedges and use the point of a small sharp knife to flick out the seeds.

Loosening the flesh from wedges This is a method of preparing melon served very simply as as an appetizer, usually plain or sprinkled with a little ground ginger or chopped candied ginger. When the seeds have been removed, cut the halves into wedges. Use a fine-bladed sharp knife to cut between the skin and the flesh of the melon, working from one end of the wedge to the other and taking care to follow the curve of the fruit to avoid leaving more than the minimum of flesh on the skin. A flexible boning knife is ideal for this.

Leave the flesh in position, then cut it across into slices. If the wedge is large, the flesh may be cut in half lengthwise before cutting across. Do not disturb the position of the flesh on the skin. Place the wedge on a serving plate.

Scooping melon balls Use a melon baller for this. These gadgets are available in two sizes. When scooping perfect melon balls, be prepared to leave about a quarter of the flesh on the skin – this can of course be eaten separately. For the majority of salads, the best compromise is to scoop out as many perfect melon balls as possible, then to scoop out those with a slightly inferior shape, leaving only a small amount of flesh on the skin. The inferior shapes can usually be mixed into a fruit salad and the better ones displayed more carefully. When making individual cocktails it is best only to use perfect balls as the appearance is marred by untidy pieces.

Halve the melon and remove the seeds, then use a baller to scoop firmly and deeply into the flesh. Work all over the melon in neat rows, starting at the top edge to extract the maximum number of well-shaped balls. This will leave a honeycomb-like network of flesh in the skin.

CITRUS FRUIT

This is one of the most significant categories of fruit in culinary terms and one which is ever-changing, with new varieties being constantly developed. The main individual types are listed in the glossary on page 118. Generally, all types are widely used in sweet and savory cooking.

The juices and natural oils contained in the peel of the fruit are called zest. This spurts from fresh fruit as the peel is cut, grated or broken. The rind is the fine outer covering on the peel – the colored part only. The pith lies between the peel and the flesh, and this varies in thickness within different varieties of the same fruit as well as between types of citrus. The flesh is divided into segments which are separated by membranes, with a tough central membrane linking the segments. Seeds usually sit at the center of the fruit, in the narrow edge of each segment. Some varieties of citrus fruit do not have seeds, notably navel oranges.

The majority of citrus fruit is coated with a fine wax to prevent loss of moisture during transportation. This wax is not harmful; however, unwaxed fruit is also available, particularly lemons, and these are usually packed in plastic bags and labeled "unwaxed".

Look for fruit which is bright, firm-skinned, and unblemished. Avoid any which is dull, with tired, slightly dried skin and browning patches.

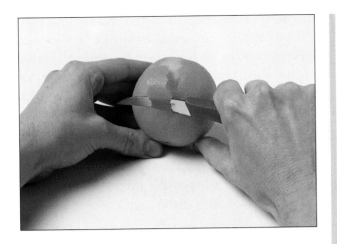

PREPARATION

Lightly scrub or thoroughly wash fruit from which the peel is to be used to remove wax and any dirt.

Paring peel Use a vegetable peeler or a fine, sharp paring knife to cut the peel off the fruit, either working around the fruit to remove a circular strip or down to remove shorter strips. Take care to cut off only the peel and not the pith. The pared peel may be cut into finer strips or chopped, or you can stamp shapes out of it using aspic cutters.

Canelle strips These are made with a canelle knife, a gadget with a small, notched blade. Working down the length of the fruit, cut off strips of peel. These are usually fairly narrow but they include more pith than strips cut from pared peel.

The technique is also used to create a decorative skin on the whole fruit by removing strips at an equal distance apart all around it. The gaps between strips should be narrow – ideally equal to the width of the strips. When the fruit is sliced the edges of the slices will have an attractive cogwheel effect.

Peeling This is particularly useful for whole oranges which are to be separated into segments for eating raw. Cut through the peel from the top to the bottom of the fruit in four or five places, then ease away a segment of peel and pith from the top so that it pulls off cleanly. Repeat to remove all the peel and pith.

Cutting off peel with all pith This is the method of peeling used when it is essential that the membrane and every trace of pith is removed from outside the fruit, for example when preparing fruit for caramelizing, or before removing individual segments.

Slice the top and bottom off the fruit, cutting away all pith so that the flesh is just visible in the middle of the slice. Use a sharp knife – preferably serrated – and stand the fruit on a board. Cut off the peel with all pith and membrane, working down the side of the fruit in neat slices. Judge the thickness of the pith and peel from the point where the flesh starts in the middle of the fruit on top. Cut off any small pieces of pith which have been missed.

Removing individual segments without membranes Peel the fruit as above, removing all pith. Hold the fruit over a basin to catch the juice which will drip away. Use a sharp, serrated knife to remove the segments. Make a first cut in as far as the middle of the fruit beside one membrane dividing two segments. When the knife reaches the middle of the fruit, sharply change its angle so that it points outward and scrape the segment free of the membrane. The first segment is the most difficult – once there is more space, it is easy to scrape off the successive segments. By first cutting then scraping, the fruit comes away without any of the tough membranes. Squeeze all juice from the membranes before discarding them.

RHUBARB

Rhubarb is the long stems of a large-leafed plant. The fruit contains natural toxins and should not be eaten in any great quantity before cooking. The leaves of the plant are poisonous.

Look for firm stems of medium size – large ones tend to be tough. Limp stems have been cut for a long time and have lost moisture.

PREPARATION

Cut off the red-colored root ends and the slightly branched shape at the top immediately below the leaf. If any tough strings show signs of coming off the stems, peel these away. Slice the fruit on a board, using a sharp knife, again pulling away any tough strings which will not readily soften during cooking.

BANANAS

Although these are most popular as a dessert fruit and as a snack, they also have a number of uses in savory cooking. The varieties are listed in the glossary on page 118, with notes on those which are used primarily for cooking.

For the best flavor, the common dessert banana should be speckled brown. Underripe bananas are green, and comparatively tasteless; they have a high starch content which is gradually converted to sugar as the fruit ripens and turns yellow. Very ripe bananas, well-speckled with brown or blackening around the edges, have a high sugar content. Over-ripe bananas have very sweet, soft flesh which many people do not particularly like; however, the fruit is still good mashed or sliced and used in cooking or combined with other dessert ingredients, such as Greek yogurt, cream, or custard.

Store bananas in a cool place. Do not keep them in a bag with other fruit as they tend to increase the speed with which other fruit ripens.

PREPARATION

Bananas discolor quickly once they are peeled, so they should be sprinkled with a little lemon juice if they are not used at once.

Mashing This is my quick method for mashing bananas: part-peel the banana, leaving enough skin in place to hold the fruit at one end. Hold the fruit on a plate and mash the peeled end onto the plate using a fork, working along the fruit and peeling back the skin as you work, until you have to remove all the banana from the skin.

PINEAPPLES

These range in size from very small fruit which are ideal for halving and serving as individual containers to medium and large fruit which will yield anything up to ten or more portions.

The color of the fruit tells you how ripe it is, from bright green when underripe, tough and extremely sharp to deep golden yellow verging on brown when overripe and well past its best. Fruit with a good yellow color is sweet and juicy with a good characteristic tang. Avoid any fruit which is overripe to the point where it has soft patches and begins to show signs of faint mold – the flesh will be brown and unpalatable.

Pineapple is widely used in savory as well as sweet cooking, with classics including ham with pineapple and sweet and sour sauce for pork. The raw fruit contains an enzyme which has a tenderizing effect on protein – poultry and meat. However, be careful not to exceed suggested marinating periods as this can result in the fruit over-tenderizing the protein and giving it an unpleasant, grainy texture. This is particularly noticeable with poultry.

The setting agent gelatin is a protein and raw pineapple will gradually reduce its setting qualities. This depends on the quantity of pineapple used – a few slices in a fruit jelly will not cause setting problems but a large quantity of raw pineapple or unpasteurized pineapple juice will. Sometimes, a fresh pineapple dessert which has set will gradually soften when left to stand for long periods (24 hours plus). In canned fruit and pasteurized juice the activity of the enzyme is stopped by heat processing.

PREPARATION

Pineapples may be halved lengthwise through the leafy top and the fruit flesh scooped out by using a knife to cut it free and a spoon to scoop it out. The shells may be used as serving containers for sweet or savory dishes.

12

Peeling Cut the top and bottom off the pineapple. Stand it on a board and use a large sharp knife to cut off the peel from top to bottom in neat strips. When all the peel is removed, use the point of a sharp knife to cut out the sharp, unpleasant spines which remain in the fruit.

Coring A slightly tough core runs down the center of the pineapple. The texture of this does vary and in some cases it may be tender enough to eat with the rest of the flesh.

To remove the core, cut the pineapple in half. Cut the core from the center of the pineapple using a sharp, fine-bladed knife, working first from one end of the fruit and cutting neatly around the core, then turning the pineapple over and working from the other end. Push the core out of the middle.

The core has a good flavor and should not be discarded; it can be diced and used in cooking.

MANGOS

The red-tinged fruit, medium or large in size, is most common but smaller yellow mangos are also available. Underripe fruit is firm and tangy; as it ripens it softens and becomes sweeter. Fruit which feels tender but not squashy and is well tinged with red (according to type) has a well-balanced flavor and flesh which is succulently tender. The flesh of very ripe fruit does not retain its shape. If the mango is red with browning patches it is overripe.

Peeling Use a vegetable peeler or sharp knife to peel the skin off the fruit, working lengthwise.

Pitting Mango pits are large and flat. Cut into the fruit from one narrow side using a fine, sharp knife. Ease the knife over the shape of the pit, then do the same from the other side to release one half of the fruit. It is then easy to cut the pit off the remaining mango half.

Cutting To slice a mango, cut in as far as the pit and down its length, then make another cut into the same central point at an angle to release a slice. Continue cutting slices off one side of the pit, then turn the fruit over to cut slices off the second side.

To remove chunks, simply make regular lengthwise cuts then cut across them to mark the size of the chunks. Cut in from one side between the chunks and the pit to separate the pieces of flesh from the pit.

Scored mango halves Halve and pit the fruit, then make evenly spaced cuts into the flesh (but not through the skin) in both directions on both halves. Push the skin from underneath to "turn the fruit inside out," which displays the scored flesh attractively and allows it to be removed easily with a spoon.

EXOTIC FRUIT

There is a wide and ever-changing range of exotic fruit on sale. The choice and preparation varies according to type, and guidance on the characteristics to look for is included in the glossary on page 118.

13

QUALITY PRODUCE

GARNISHES & DECORATIONS

The range of fruit garnishes and decorations is wide. The following list encompasses some popular ideas.

Fruit slices Slices of fruit make the simplest of garnishes and decorations for both savory and sweet dishes. With a sharp knife, cut thin, even slices. Use them whole or halved. Citrus fruit, apples with bright peel, Chinese gooseberries, star fruit, mango, and peach are a few examples of fruit that makes an attractive garnish.

Citrus twists Cut thin slices, then make a slit into the center of each. Move the slit in the fruit in opposite directions to stand the slice up and form the twist.

Fruit wedges Lemons, limes, oranges, apples, peaches, plums, and apricots are all suitable. Cut wedges neatly and arrange them in pairs or threes, lying on their sides or standing neatly.

Vandyke cut This is used to halve the fruit. It is popular for citrus fruit and may also be used for other fruit such as small melons.

Use a fine-bladed, sharp knife. Make a cut half-way down the length of the fruit in as far as the center and at a slight angle. Remove the knife and make another cut in the same way only at the opposite angle to create a "V" shape. Continue cutting all around the middle of the fruit, linking all the "V" cuts to halve the fruit. Gently pull the halves apart.

Butterflies Cut thin citrus fruit slices and make slits from opposite sides into the middle but not right to the center, so that the slices remain in one piece. Trim the edges of the cuts, then twist them in opposite directions to make butterfly shapes.

Sliced fruit fans Prepare and thinly slice the fruit into neat, even pieces. As you work, keep the slices together as far as possible in the original form of the fruit. Lift the slices together onto the plate then gently fan them out, using the point of a knife to ease the pieces neatly into position. Pears, lime halves, star fruit, mango halves, and peaches are a few examples of fruit to fan. Strawberries make excellent fans – leave their stems on and the slices slightly attached together at the stem end.

Fruit and leaves Arrange bunches of currants, fruit fans or frosted fruit with edible leaves as a decoration or garnish. Mint, nasturtium, and lemon balm leaves are all suitable. Non-poisonous inedible leaves such as geranium leaves may also be used.

Frosted fruit Brush small whole fruit or pieces of fruit with a little lightly whisked egg white, then coat with superfine sugar. Strawberries, bunches of currants, kumquats and mandarin segments are all suitable.

Citrus peel decorations Pare the peel (see page 11) and cut or stamp out shapes. Alternatively, cut very fine strips. Cook the shapes in a little simmering water for 5–10 minutes until softened, then drain and use as required. Leaves, aspic cutter shapes, and small mounds of fine strips can be made by this method.

15

FRUIT JUICES

ORANGE TODDY

HOT LEMON & HONEY

BANANA SHAKE

PEACH MILK SHAKE

PEAR & PASSION COCKTAIL

GUAVA YOGURT REFRESHER

JAMAICAN RUMBA

SUMMER FRUIT CUP

MANGO FRAPPÉ

PEACH DREAM

PAPAYA SUNSET

WATERMELON COOLER

FRESH LEMON DRINK

SANGRIA

CUT CITRUS FRUITS in half and squeeze them by hand with a lemon squeezer, or peel the fruit and put it in a blender (see Lemon Drink on page 23).

Soft fruits can be blended with sugar and water with a squeeze of lemon juice to bring out the flavor.

Sodas are fruit drinks which are different and quite filling. They are made with blended fruit and water or milk, depending on the type of fruit. Mangoes, milk, and crushed ice make a delicious drink.

Interesting combinations of exotic fruits can be made into drinks, for example peach and papaya, mango and papaya, strawberry and orange, passion fruit and banana, orange and grapefruit, orange and lemon, ginger and lime.

When serving long drinks in hot weather, use lots of fruit garnishes creatively, either in a punch bowl or on the side of a glass, making colorful and appealing drinks. Use either whole or sliced fruits and flowers in ice cubes for an interesting effect.

Tea, a stimulating drink on its own, can be used as a base for fruit punches and many other fruit drinks. There are also many varieties of fruit tea available, either as loose tea or tea bags. These may be served either hot or cold, with or without added alcohol.

18

Left: Orange Toddy **Right:** Hot Lemon and Honey

ORANGE TODDY

INGREDIENTS

SERVES 2

1 large orange

1 tbsp. clear honey

¾ cup water

⅔ cup dark rum

METHOD

Thinly peel the skin from the orange. Place the peel, honey, and water in a small saucepan. Simmer for 5 minutes to extract flavor from the orange peel. Add the rum, heat slightly and then strain into 2 mugs.

HOT LEMON & HONEY

INGREDIENTS

SERVES 2

juice of 1 lemon

4 tbsp. honey

2 cups boiling water

METHOD

Divide the lemon and honey between 2 mugs, gradually pour on boiling water and stir to dissolve the honey.

Drink as hot as possible. If liked, add 1 tablespoon of whisky.

Left: *Banana Shake* **Right:** *Peach Milk Shake*

BANANA SHAKE

INGREDIENTS

1¼ cups cold milk

1 small banana

1 tbsp. sugar

2 tbsp. extra-thick heavy cream

½ tsp. sweetened chocolate powder

METHOD

Place the cold milk in a blender. Peel the banana, slice and add to the milk with the sugar. Process for 1 minute and divide between 2 glasses.

Mix the cream and chocolate powder together in a small bowl, and place a spoonful on the top of each drink.

PEACH MILK SHAKE

INGREDIENTS

3 small peaches

1¼ cups milk

1 tbsp. superfine sugar

1 tbsp. apricot or peach brandy (optional)

grated chocolate, to decorate

METHOD

Skin, halve and pit the peaches. Cut each into four, place in a blender with the remaining ingredients and process until smooth.

Chill and serve with a little grated chocolate on top.

PEAR & PASSION COCKTAIL

INGREDIENTS

1 ripe pear

¼ cup vodka

1 passion fruit

5 tbsp. light cream

1 tsp. honey

carbonated water

floral cubes (see page 18), to garnish

METHOD

Peel and core the pear and place the flesh in a blender with the vodka and passion fruit. Process and strain through a fine strainer into a measuring jug. Add the cream and honey, stir and add sufficient carbonated water to make 1¼ cups.

Pour into 2 glasses and garnish each with a floral ice cube. Alternatively, use an ordinary ice cube with a sprig of borage or nasturtium flowers.

Left: *Guava Yoghurt Refresher* **Right:** *Mango Frappé*

GUAVA YOGURT REFRESHER

INGREDIENTS

8 oz. fresh guava

2½ cups natural yogurt

1¼ cups tonic water

2 tsp. lemon or lime juice

sugar to taste

cucumber, to garnish (optional)

SERVES 4~6

METHOD

Peel and quarter the guava, remove the coarse seeds in the center, and place it in a blender with the yogurt. Process, then pour into a pitcher.

Add the tonic water, lemon or lime juice, and sugar to taste.

Serve well chilled. Garnish with cucumber, if liked.

JAMAICAN RUMBA

INGREDIENTS

1 × 2 inch slice fresh pineapple, skin removed

1 oz. piece creamed coconut

5 tbsp. white rum

1 small banana, peeled

2 tsp. clear honey

2 cups milk

crushed ice, to serve

To garnish

sliced pineapple

sliced banana

METHOD

Place all the ingredients, except the ice and garnish, in a blender and process until smooth. Taste and add extra rum if preferred.

Serve chilled with crushed ice and garnish each glass with sliced banana and pineapple.

SUMMER FRUIT CUP

This is a delicious, refreshing summer drink. Borage leaves add a refreshing, cucumber-like flavor.

INGREDIENTS

2 bottles dry or medium dry white wine

3–4 tbsp. Maraschino or Cointreau liqueur

2½ cups tonic water

2 cups lemonade

1 orange

1 lemon or lime

1 cup strawberries

young borage leaves

METHOD

Place all the liquids in a large pitcher. Thinly slice the orange, lemon or lime, and strawberries and add to the liquid. Wash the borage leaves and add. Chill for at least 1 hour before serving.

MANGO FRAPPÉ

INGREDIENTS

1 large ripe mango

5 ice cubes, crushed

2 tsp. sugar

2½ cups sparkling Chardonnay

mango slices to garnish

METHOD

Cut the flesh from the mango, cut 3 or 4 thin slices for the garnish then place the remaining flesh in a blender with the crushed ice and sugar. Process until smooth. Strain into a serving pitcher, pour in the Chardonnay, stir and serve at once, garnished with the reserved slices. *See picture opposite.*

Left: **Peach Dream** *Right:* **Papaya Sunset**

22

PEACH DREAM

INGREDIENTS

1 ripe peach, peeled

1¼ cups medium dry white wine, well chilled

1 tbsp. brandy

sugar to taste (optional)

flowers, to garnish

METHOD

Remove the pit from the peach, chop the flesh, and place in a blender with the wine and brandy. Process, adding sugar if liked. Strain into glasses and garnish with flowers.

PAPAYA SUNSET

INGREDIENTS

½ medium-sized papaya

juice of ½ lime

juice of 1 orange

3 tbsp. Grand Marnier

⅔ cup ginger ale

ice cubes

To garnish

slices of lime

slices of orange

METHOD

Peel the papaya and scoop out the seeds. Chop the flesh and place it in a blender with the lime and orange juice, process and strain into a serving pitcher. Stir in the Grand Marnier and add the ginger ale.

Serve each with an ice cube and garnish with slices of orange and lime.

WATERMELON COOLER

INGREDIENTS

½ small watermelon
sugar to taste

METHOD

Cut the watermelon into quarters and scoop out the flesh, removing the seeds.

Place the watermelon in a blender and process until smooth, adding a little sugar, which sweetens the flavor and strengthens the color.

Strain into a pitcher and chill well before serving.

FRESH LEMON DRINK

This recipe can also be made with oranges and limes, although you would need twice the amount of limes as they are so small.

INGREDIENTS

4 large lemons
sugar to taste
2½ cups boiling water
ice cubes

METHOD

Thinly peel the rind from 2 lemons and place it in a measuring jug. Add 2 tbsp. sugar and pour on boiling water. Stir to dissolve the sugar, leave to cool.

Remove the lemon peel and discard. Squeeze the juice from the 4 lemons and strain it into a large pitcher. Add the infused liquid, taste and add ice cubes and water to a suitable dilution. Add extra sugar if required.

Note: If using limes, choose the largest you can find and use 6–8, but reduce the amount of peel to be infused as too much will make the drink bitter.

SANGRIA

Makes 4 ¼ cups

You can make this drink extra-appealing by using floral or fruity ice cubes or borage leaves if available.

INGREDIENTS

1 pear, sliced
2 peaches or nectarines, peeled and sliced
2 Chinese gooseberries
1 ripe star fruit
1 cup cherries, pitted
1 orange, thinly peeled
1 lemon, thinly peeled
4 ¼ cups dry red wine
1 cinnamon stick
⅔ cup brandy
1 ¼ cups soda water
sugar to taste
ice cubes

METHOD

Place the pear, peaches or nectarines in a large pitcher. Skin the Chinese gooseberries, chop the flesh and add to the pitcher. Slice the star fruit and add with the cherries and orange and lemon peel. Segment the orange, chop and add with the red wine and cinnamon stick. Leave to stand for 1 hour.

Add the brandy, soda water, sugar to taste, and top up with ice cubes.

CHAPTER TWO

FULL OF SUNSHINE

EXOTIC MUESLI

BREAKFAST CRUNCH

RASPBERRY OATIE

TAMARILLO &
AVOCADO COCKTAIL

PAPAYA &
STRAWBERRY SALAD

AVOCADO & APPLE SALAD

SPINACH & FIG SALAD

STUFFED FIGS WITH PLUMS

STAR FRUIT & ROCKET SALAD
WITH RASPBERRY VINEGAR
DRESSING

APPLE & ROLLMOP
SMØRREBRØD

WALDORF & BASIL RICE

LIME BUTTER WITH ASPARAGUS

FROMAGE FRAIS WITH
PASSION FRUIT

THESE DISHES MAKE a new approach to starting the day, or brunch if breakfast has been in too much of a rush. You will also find a choice of healthy dishes for lunchtime which are so versatile they could also be served as appetizers for a dinner party, or used as side dishes to accompany a main dish.

Fruit and nuts may be varied according to availability. For example, in the recipe for fromage frais with passion fruit, macadamia nuts could be used instead of cashews.

EXOTIC MUESLI

INGREDIENTS

6 tbsp. thick yogurt

6 tbsp. rolled oats

1 large mango

2 bananas

3 Chinese gooseberries

2 tbsp. brown sugar

1 tbsp. Brazil nuts, chopped

SERVES 4~6

METHOD

Place the yogurt in a bowl with the rolled oats. Prepare and add the mango. Peel and slice the bananas and Chinese gooseberries, and add to the bowl. Sprinkle with brown sugar and chopped nuts.

BREAKFAST CRUNCH

INGREDIENTS

SERVES 4~6

¼ cup sunflower seeds

¼ cup pine kernels

¼ cup sesame seeds

2 oranges

2 tbsp. brown sugar

½ cup dried figs, chopped

2 large bananas

2½ cups Greek yogurt

METHOD

Using a dry skillet, roast the sunflower seeds and pine kernels for 3 minutes over a moderate heat, then add the sesame seeds and roast for a further 3 minutes, stirring to give even browning. Remove the pan from the heat.

Coarsely grate the peel from 1 orange and add to the pan with the sugar and dried figs. Stir until well combined and cook for 2 minutes. Leave to cool.

Remove the peel and pith from the oranges and cut them into pieces. Slice the bananas and mix with the oranges and yogurt, divide between 4 dishes and top each with the fig mixture. Serve at once.

RASPBERRY OATIE

INGREDIENTS

2¼ cups raspberries

1 tbsp. superfine sugar

3 tbsp. butter

1½ tbsp. soft brown sugar

¾ cup quick-cook porridge oats

SERVES 4

METHOD

Preheat the oven to 425°.

Divide the raspberries into 4 individual ovenproof dishes and sprinkle each with a little superfine sugar. Melt the butter and brown sugar in a saucepan and stir in the oats. Cook for 2–3 minutes and then divide between each portion of raspberries, spreading evenly with a fork. Place in the oven for 10 minutes. Serve either hot or cold with yogurt.

TAMARILLO & AVOCADO COCKTAIL

INGREDIENTS

2 large ripe avocados

3 tamarillos

shredded lettuce

½ cup soft cheese with herbs and garlic

6 tbsp. Greek yogurt or sour cream

1 tsp. superfine sugar

3 scallions or green onions, chopped

SERVES
4

METHOD

Quarter and peel the avocados and slice them across. Peel the tamarillos thinly, halve them lengthwise and slice across. Arrange a little shredded lettuce on 4 individual plates.

Mix the cheese with the yogurt or sour cream in a bowl. Sprinkle the superfine sugar over the tamarillos, mix in the chopped scallion and leave to stand for 15 minutes.

Arrange the avocado slices on the lettuce, top with the tamarillo mixture and spoon the cheese and yogurt dressing over the top.

PAPAYA & STRAWBERRY SALAD

INGREDIENTS
1 medium-sized ripe papaya

1 cup fresh strawberries, hulled

3 inch piece cucumber

6 tbsp. orange dressing (see page 96)

watercress, to garnish

SERVES 4

METHOD
Cut the papaya into four, remove the skin and seeds, and slice the flesh into a serving dish. Cut the strawberries into quarters or halves, if large, and add to the papaya. Peel the cucumber and cut into slices. Add to the fruits with the dressing. Toss gently and serve slightly chilled, garnished with watercress.

AVOCADO & APPLE SALAD

INGREDIENTS
SERVES 4

2 ripe avocado pears

2 small eating apples

4 tbsp. vinaigrette dressing (see page 97)

1 tbsp. freshly chopped parsley

METHOD
Peel off the green skins of the avocados, cut in half and remove the pits. Slice the flesh thinly and place in a bowl. Wash the apples, quarter and core, dice and add to the avocado with the dressing and chopped parsley.

SPINACH & FIG SALAD

INGREDIENTS

1 lb. fresh spinach, washed

¼ cup pine kernels

3 fresh figs

4 tbsp. lemon dressing

a few fresh nasturtium flowers (optional)

SERVES 4

METHOD

Remove and discard any coarse stems from the spinach and tear the leaves into pieces. Place in a colander to drain well. Place the pine kernels in a small, dry pan and roast until lightly browned, stirring all the time. Remove from the pan and leave to cool.

Wash the figs, trim off the stems, cut each into quarters and then into thin slices. Place the spinach, pine kernels and figs into a serving bowl. Sprinkle over the dressing, toss well and garnish with a few fresh nasturtium flowers, if available.

STUFFED FIGS WITH PLUMS

This can be made with apricots, small pears or other suitable fruits that are not too large.

INGREDIENTS

½ cup chopped almonds

4 oz. lean bacon

½ cup cream cheese

1 tbsp. chopped chives

freshly ground pepper

4 figs

8 plums

lollo rosso lettuce, to garnish

METHOD

Place the almonds either in a dry skillet or in a broiler pan, with the rack removed, and toast to brown lightly. Remove and cool.

Fry or broil the bacon until crisp, drain on paper towels and chop into pieces. Soften the cheese in a bowl and add the almonds, bacon, chives, and pepper.

Cut the stems off the figs and cut down into each fig twice, not cutting completely through. Open out so that there are 4 wedges. Place a fig on each of 4 plates and put a little of the cheese mixture in the center of each fruit. Cut the plums in half, remove the pits and divide the remaining cheese mixture between them. Arrange 4 halves round each fig and garnish with a little lollo rosso lettuce.

STARFRUIT & ROCKET SALAD WITH RASPBERRY VINEGAR DRESSING

This makes a very good side salad or appetizer. Rocket has a strong, very distinctive flavor which is excellent when balanced with sweet salad greens such as iceburg or cos lettuce, but do not be tempted to add too much rocket or cut it too coarsely as it will overpower the other delicate ingredients, especially the star fruit. If rocket is not available a bunch or two of watercress may be used instead.

INGREDIENTS
½ iceburg lettuce, shredded

12 medium rocket leaves, finely shredded

3 scallions or green onions, chopped

2 star fruit, sliced and quartered

SERVES 4

For the dressing

3 tbsp. raspberry vinegar (see page 107)

1 tsp. superfine sugar

salt and freshly ground black pepper

8 tbsp. olive oil

METHOD

Toss the lettuce, rocket and scallions together in a salad bowl. Next make the dressing: place the vinegar in a basin and whisk in the superfine sugar with plenty of seasoning. Continue whisking until the sugar and salt have dissolved. Slowly add the olive oil, whisking all the time to combine the ingredients well.

Add the star fruit to the salad. Pour the dressing over and mix lightly. Serve at once. Do not leave the star fruit to stand for any length of time once it is cut as it dries on the surface and tends to discolor slightly around the edges.

APPLE & ROLLMOP SMØRREBRØD

Danish sandwiches are quick and easy to make. All kinds of toppings may be used and a variety of breads for the base. Be adventurous and use exotic fruits for flavor and color. These can be used with both meat and cheese to make an appealing snack or appetizer.

INGREDIENTS

6 thin slices of brown, white or rye bread

butter for spreading

6 pickled rollmop herrings

2 large eating apples

4 tbsp. sour cream

2 tbsp. mayonnaise

freshly ground pepper

fresh dill, fennel or parsley

METHOD

Spread the bread slices thickly with butter and cut each slice in half. Unroll the rollmops and cut each across into 6 pieces, removing the tails. Arrange 3 pieces on each piece of bread.

Wash the apples, remove the cores and cut the flesh into dice. Place in a bowl. Mix in the sour cream, mayonnaise, and pepper and divide between the slices, arranging neatly on top. Garnish with one of the fresh herbs.

Note: Try pork with mango or orange; salami with papaya; chicken with curry and grapefruit; cream cheese with Chinese gooseberry and passion fruit; and cream with strawberry, Chinese gooseberry, or banana.

WALDORF & BASIL RICE

INGREDIENTS

generous ½ cup basmati rice

salt

6 large fresh basil leaves, shredded

1 tbsp. olive oil

1 tsp. cider vinegar

freshly ground black pepper

1½ cups finely shredded white or red cabbage

½ cup walnuts, chopped

½ small onion, finely chopped

⅓ cup golden raisins

3 eating apples, washed and cored

6 tbsp. mayonnaise

3 tbsp Greek yogurt

extra basil leaves, to garnish

METHOD

Put the rice into a pan of boiling, salted water, and simmer for 15 minutes. Drain and rinse well, then drain again.

Mix the basil, oil, cider vinegar, and some black pepper together and stir into the cooked rice. Leave to marinate for 30 minutes.

Place the cabbage in a bowl with the walnuts, onion, and golden raisins. Keeping half an apple on one side, dice the remainder and add to the bowl. Mix the mayonnaise and yogurt together and stir into the salad.

Put the rice in a dish with the salad arranged in the center. Garnish with the reserved apple, sliced, and the basil leaves.

LIME BUTTER WITH ASPARAGUS

This is very quick and simple to make, but the butter should be at room temperature to be successful. Other vegetables with which this is delicious are Swiss chard, salsify, and globe artichokes.

INGREDIENTS

½ cup softened butter

freshly ground white pepper

finely grated peel of 1 lime

juice of ½ lime

salt

METHOD

Beat the butter with a slightly wet warm metal spoon until it is light and fluffy. Continue beating, adding the pepper, grated lime peel and lime juice. Season with salt if necessary. Cook the asparagus in boiling salted water until just tender. Serve hot with the lime butter spooned over.

FROMAGE FRAIS WITH PASSION FRUIT

A refreshing snack that is quick to prepare and nutritious.

INGREDIENTS

SERVES 3~4

1 cup fromage frais

2–3 passion fruit

½ cup cashew nuts

sugar to taste (optional)

lettuce and cucumber, to garnish

METHOD

Place the fromage frais in a bowl. Halve the passion fruit and stir in with the nuts. Add sugar, if liked. Spoon into 4 lettuce leaves garnished with cucumber and serve with warm brown rolls.

MAIN DISH MEDLEY

**LEMON & LIME
SEAFOOD SALAD**

**MACKEREL IN OATMEAL WITH
RED CURRANT SAUCE**

SHRIMP & PAPAYA PANCAKES

CHICKEN MARYLAND

GUAVA & TURKEY KEBABS

**CHICKEN SALAD WITH
CHERRIES & TARRAGON**

**TURKEY ROAST WITH
CRANBERRIES**

**SWEET & SOUR CHICKEN WITH
PERSIMMON**

**VENISON CASSEROLE WITH
RED CURRANTS**

ROAST PORK WITH WHOLE FRUITS

PORKBURGERS WITH PINEAPPLE

JAMBALAYA

RABBIT WITH WILD BERRY SAUCE

CURRIED LAMB WITH APRICOTS

DUCK GALANTINE WITH ORANGE

SPICED BACON CASSEROLE

**BEEF CASSEROLE WITH
KUMQUATS**

LEMON & LIME SEAFOOD SALAD

This is a fresh-tasting fish salad. The choice of fish and herbs can be varied according to taste.

INGREDIENTS

SERVES 4

1 lb. fresh haddock

2 fresh scallops

½ lb. sword fish or similar fish

6 oz. prepared fresh squid

1 cup fresh shelled shrimp

6 tbsp. chopped fresh parsley

2 tbsp. chopped fresh tarragon

4 tbsp. chopped fresh mint

3 tbsp. olive oil

juice of 1 lemon

juice of 1 lime

bunch of scallions or green onions, trimmed and chopped

salt and freshly ground pepper

METHOD

Clean and skin the haddock and cut into small pieces. Clean the scallops. Bone and cube the sword fish. Wash the squid and cut into rings. Poach all together in lightly salted water for a short time until just cooked. Drain well, cool and place in a mixing bowl with the shelled shrimp.

Place all the herbs in a bowl with the oil, citrus juices, scallions, salt and freshly ground pepper. Stir round and pour over the fish and lightly toss. Leave for approximately 30 minutes for the flavors to develop.

Serve with a rice salad and sliced tomatoes and, if liked, garlic bread.

MACKEREL IN OATMEAL WITH RED CURRANT SAUCE

INGREDIENTS

4 small mackerel

salt and pepper

1 cup medium oatmeal

6 tbsp. butter

1 tbsp. oil

For the sauce

2 cups fresh red currants, stringed

6 tbsp. water

2–4 tbsp. sugar

¼ tsp. ground allspice

METHOD

Remove the heads from the mackerel. Wash the mackerel, dry on paper towels, season with salt and pepper and dip in the oatmeal. Leave on one side.

To make the sauce, cook the red currants in the water until soft. Add the sugar and allspice, and cook to thicken a little.

Melt the butter and oil in a skillet, add the mackerel and cook for about 5 minutes, then turn and cook for a further 5–10 minutes, depending on the thickness of the mackerel. The mackerel should be crisp and golden. Serve the sauce separately.

SHRIMP & PAPAYA PANCAKES

INGREDIENTS

For the pancake batter

1 cup all-purpose flour

1 egg

dash of salt

1 tbsp. corn oil

1¼ cups milk

vegetable oil for frying

For the filling

1 lb. shrimp in shells

1 medium-sized papaya

3 tbsp. sweet butter

1 small leek, trimmed and thinly sliced

2 inch piece fresh ginger, grated

2 tbsp. dry martini

1 tbsp. lime juice (optional)

salt and freshly ground white pepper

1 cup crème fraîche

2–3 tbsp. chopped fresh dill or fennel

SERVES 4–5

METHOD

Make the pancakes by beating the flour, egg, salt, and oil together then gradually beating in the milk. This quantity should make 8–10 fairly small, thin pancakes. Heat a little oil in a small skillet and pour in sufficient mixture to cover thinly. Cook both sides of the pancakes. Keep hot until all the batter has been used.

Shell the shrimp. Peel the papaya, halve them and remove the seeds then cut the flesh into fairly small dice. Melt the butter in a skillet. Add the leek, cook until slightly soft, add the ginger and cook for a few seconds. Add the martini, shrimp, and papaya to the pan with the lime juice, if used, and salt and pepper. Heat through gently.

Fold each pancake into 4 and, dividing the filling between the pancakes, use a pocket of each pancake to hold the filling. Place on a heated dish and put in a warm oven until ready to serve.

Mix the crème fraîche with the dill or fennel, add salt and pepper to taste and serve with the pancakes.

CHICKEN MARYLAND

This is a traditional recipe served with corn fritters, bacon rolls, and apple bananas.

INGREDIENTS

2 whole boned chicken breasts

1 egg, well beaten

fresh bread crumbs

oil for frying

8 bacon slices

4 firm apple bananas

For the corn fritters

¾ cup all-purpose flour

salt and pepper

1 egg

4 tbsp. milk

1 small can corn kernels, drained

parsley, chopped

sweet butter for frying

parsley or watercress, to garnish

METHOD

Remove the skin from the chicken breasts. Dip the chicken in the beaten egg and coat evenly with bread crumbs, pressing them on with a metal spatula. Leave to one side.

Heat ½ inch oil in a skillet and cook the chicken breasts quickly until they are brown, turning once. Reduce the heat and cook for 12–15 minutes until cooked through. Remove and keep hot.

Meanwhile, remove the rind from the bacon, roll the bacon up and thread on to a skewer. Place on the broiler rack and cook under a moderate broiler until slightly crisp. Remove and keep hot.

Make the fritters by placing the flour, seasoning, and egg in a bowl, gradually adding the milk and beating well to make a smooth batter. Add the drained corn and the chopped parsley.

Melt a little butter in a shallow skillet and drop in tablespoons of the fritter mixture. Fry quickly for about 2 minutes on each side. This will make 8 fritters. Remove and keep hot.

Peel the bananas. Add to the skillet, adding a little more butter if necessary, and cook for about 1 minute to heat through and lightly brown all over.

Place the chicken breasts on a heated serving dish. Garnish each with a banana, the bacon rolls, and the corn fritters arranged round the edge. Garnish with parsley or watercress.

41

GUAVA & TURKEY KEBABS

These kebabs have a delicate flavor. Chicken could be substituted for the turkey.

INGREDIENTS

6 tbsp. olive oil

3 tbsp. lemon or lime juice

2 cloves garlic, crushed

2 tsp. soy sauce

freshly ground pepper

3 tbsp. chopped chives

1 lb. turkey breasts

12 oz. guavas

METHOD

Place the oil, lemon or lime juice, garlic, soy sauce, pepper, and chives in a shallow dish large enough to take the turkey. Cut the turkey into pieces suitable to go on to skewers and place in the marinade. Cover and leave to marinate for several hours, turning occasionally.

Peel and quarter the guavas, remove the coarse seeds in the center and cut into bite-sized pieces. Divide the turkey and guava pieces between 4 skewers, alternating with 2 pieces of turkey to 1 piece of guava.

Place on a broiler rack and cook under a moderate heat, basting with the remaining marinade, for 12–15 minutes until the turkey is cooked through.

Serve with a herbed, buttered rice and a light salad.

CHICKEN SALAD WITH CHERRIES & TARRAGON

A rice salad makes a good accompaniment to this dish.

INGREDIENTS

⅔ cup real mayonnaise

⅓ cup Greek yogurt

a good tbsp. freshly chopped tarragon

freshly ground white pepper

dash of salt

1¼ lb. cooked chicken, diced

2 cups fresh cherries, pitted

extra tarragon leaves, to garnish

METHOD

Mix the mayonnaise in a bowl with the yogurt, chopped tarragon, pepper, and salt. Leave for 30 minutes for the flavors to combine.

Add the chicken and stir so that the chicken is coated in the dressing. Stir in the cherries just before serving and garnish with the extra tarragon.

TURKEY ROAST WITH CRANBERRIES

This recipe may be made in advance and frozen but must be completely thawed before cooking.

INGREDIENTS

6 slices fresh turkey breasts, approximately 1¾ lb.

6 bacon slices, rind removed

For the forcemeat stuffing

¼ cup finely chopped onion

2 cups fresh bread crumbs

2 tbsp. butter, melted

1 egg, well beaten

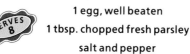

1 tbsp. chopped fresh parsley

salt and pepper

For the sausage meat stuffing

1 cup pork sausage meat

¼ cup finely chopped onion

½ cup fresh bread crumbs

1 cup fresh cranberries

METHOD

Preheat the oven to 400°

Make the forcemeat stuffing by mixing the onion, bread crumbs, butter, egg, parsley, salt and pepper together. Then make the sausage meat stuffing by mixing all the ingredients together.

Place 2 turkey breast slices on a large piece of foil, spread half of the forcemeat stuffing and half of the sausage meat stuffing on top. Cover this with 2 more turkey breast slices. Cover these with the remainder of the stuffings and cover with the remaining 2 turkey breasts. Mold together to give a turkey breast shape. Place the bacon slices over the top of the joint and tie in several places with string to give a neat shape.

Wrap the joint in the foil, place it in a roasting pan for ease of lifting out, and cook in the oven for 1¾ hours. Serve hot with gravy, roast potatoes, cranberry and orange sauce, bread sauce, and green vegetables.

SWEET & SOUR CHICKEN WITH PERSIMMON

INGREDIENTS

2 half chicken breasts, skinned

3 tbsp. sweet butter

½ medium-sized leek, washed and thinly sliced

1 tsp. grated fresh ginger

SERVES 2

1 persimmon

1 tbsp. light soft brown sugar

salt and pepper

2 tsp. lemon juice

METHOD

Cut each chicken breast into 3 or 4 pieces. Melt the butter and quickly fry the chicken to brown each side. Remove to a plate.

Stir in the leek and cook slowly for about 2 minutes to soften slightly without browning. Add the ginger, return the chicken to the pan and cook slowly for 10–12 minutes to cook through.

Peel the persimmon, removing any pits, and cut the flesh into slices. Add to the pan with the sugar, salt and pepper, and lemon juice to taste. Heat the fruit through and serve with a crisp green vegetable and sauté potatoes.

VENISON CASSEROLE WITH RED CURRANTS

This casserole needs to be marinated overnight to impart flavor and tenderize the fibers. Traditionally, red currant jelly is served with venison or is included in an accompanying sauce. Adding the fruit during cooking and rounding off the finished dish gives a slightly sharp, sweet flavor. You can use frozen red currants if fresh are unavailable.

INGREDIENTS

2 lb. lean venison, cubed

1¼ cups red wine

1 onion, chopped

2 sprigs rosemary

3 tbsp. olive oil

10 juniper berries, slightly crushed

3 small carrots, peeled and sliced

finely grated peel of 1 orange

2 tbsp. sweet butter

6 oz. pickling onions, peeled and left whole

½ orange pepper, sliced

3 tbsp. soft brown sugar

1½ cups red currants, stringed

1 tbsp. all-purpose flour

METHOD

Place the venison, wine, onion, rosemary, oil, juniper berries, carrots, and orange peel in an ovenproof casserole. Stir, cover and leave in a cool place overnight (or longer for a more gamey flavor), stirring occasionally.

Preheat the oven to 350°. Cook for 2½ hours, reducing the oven temperature after 1 hour to 325°.

Melt the butter in a saucepan, add the pickling onions and cook for about 10 minutes until lightly browned. Add the pepper and cook for 5 minutes, stirring. Cover and then cook gently for 10 minutes.

Add the soft brown sugar and 1 cup red currants and cook until reduced to a pulp. Cool slightly. Add the flour and stir to make a thick paste, then stir in a ladleful of liquid from the venison to give a smooth consistency. Pour the mixture into the casserole and stir well. Return to the oven for a further 30 minutes.

Finally, add the remaining red currants to the casserole, taste for seasoning and sweetness and cook for an additional 5 minutes.

Serve with rice or noodles and a crisp side salad.

44

ROAST PORK WITH WHOLE FRUITS

INGREDIENTS

3 lb. blade Boston roast

a little oil

salt

2 eating apples

2 pears

2 peaches or nectarines

⅔ cup cider

⅔ cup stock or water and ½ bouillon cube

3 tbsp. all-purpose flour

2 tbsp. Calvados

2 tbsp. red currant jelly

freshly ground pepper

METHOD

Preheat the oven to 375°.

Weigh the joint and calculate the cooking time at 30 minutes to 1 lb. and 30 minutes over. Brush the pork rind with a little oil and sprinkle lightly with salt. Place the joint on a trivet in a roasting pan and roast for 30 minutes. Reduce the oven temperature to 350° and roast for a further 60 minutes.

Wash the apples and pears, cut into quarters and remove the cores. Skin the peaches and cut into halves, removing pits.

Remove the joint from the oven and pour off and reserve the fat. Place the fruit under the trivet in the roasting pan, pour in the cider, return to the oven and cook for a further 30 minutes until the fruit is tender.

Place the joint on a heated serving plate with the fruit, pour the liquid from the roasting pan into a measuring jug and make up to 1¼ cups with stock or water and bouillon cube.

Measure 3 tbsp. of the pork fat into a small saucepan, stir in the flour, add the Calvados, cook for 1 minute and gradually stir in the stock. Bring to a boil, stirring, and cook for 2 minutes. Stir in the red currant jelly and season with pepper to taste. Strain before serving.

Serve with roast potatoes and a green vegetable.

PORKBURGERS WITH PINEAPPLE

INGREDIENTS

SERVES 4

2 cups ground pork

1 tsp. dried sage

4 scallions or green onions, chopped

1 cup fresh brown bread crumbs

salt and pepper

1 egg

1 tbsp. brown sugar

2 tbsp. cider or apple juice

4 slices fresh pineapple

METHOD

Mix the pork with the sage, onions, bread crumbs, seasoning, and egg. Knead the mixture so that it binds together. Shape into 4 burgers.

Heat a heavy-based pan and cook the burgers until they are brown on both sides and cooked through, about 8–10 minutes. Transfer to a heated serving dish. Add the sugar, cider or apple juice to the juices in the pan. Heat through until the sugar dissolves, bring to a boil and then add the pineapple slices. Cook until the pineapple is glazed in the juices. Put a pineapple slice on top of each burger. Serve with mashed potatoes and a green salad.

JAMBALAYA

INGREDIENTS

3 tbsp. olive oil

½ lb. lean pork, cut into cubes

1 small red pepper, seeded and sliced

1 onion, chopped

1 chorizo sausage, sliced

generous ½ cup long-grain rice

½ tsp. ground ginger

¼ tsp. turmeric

¼ tsp. paprika

salt and freshly ground black pepper

lemon juice

1 ¼ cups chicken stock

1 ⅓ cups cooked shelled shrimp

3 slices fresh pineapple, cut into segments

SERVES
4

METHOD

Heat the olive oil in a large skillet and fry the pork fairly quickly until evenly browned. Using a slotted spoon, remove the meat to a plate. Add the pepper and onion and cook gently to soften. Add the sausage and the rice and stir until the rice becomes opaque. Turn the heat down and return the pork to the pan. Add the spices, seasoning, a little lemon juice and the chicken stock. Simmer gently until the stock is absorbed and the rice cooked. Stir in the shrimp and pineapple and heat through.

RABBIT WITH WILD BERRY SAUCE

The sauce that accompanies this dish can be made when the fruits are in season and frozen for use later. It is not a preserve. It is deliciously tangy and would go with other meats such as venison, pork, turkey, hare, and duck.

INGREDIENTS

1 rabbit, jointed
2 tbsp. Dijon mustard
6 bacon slices
For the marinade
6 black peppercorns
1 bay leaf
2 sprigs parsley
1 onion, sliced
2 tbsp. olive oil
1 cup dry white wine
For the sauce
3 cups blackberries
1 cup blueberries
⅓ cup white malt vinegar
¼ cup golden granulated sugar
¼ tsp. ground cinnamon
½ tsp. ground allspice
1 tbsp. cornstarch
1 tbsp. water

METHOD

Place the rabbit in a large dish in a single layer. Place the marinade ingredients in a saucepan and heat gently until almost boiling. Remove from the heat and cool before pouring over the rabbit. Leave to marinate for about 12 hours.

Remove the rabbit, reserving the marinade. Spread a little mustard on each piece of rabbit and wrap a bacon slice around each piece.

Preheat the oven to 350°. Place the rabbit in a roasting pan and cook for about 1 hour or until it is tender, basting occasionally.

Meanwhile, make the sauce. Place all the ingredients except the cornstarch and water in a saucepan. Cook until the fruit has softened and the liquid reduced a little. Blend the cornstarch with the water. Stir into the pan and cook for about 2 minutes until thickened and clear.

Remove the rabbit pieces from the oven, place on a warm serving dish and keep hot. Strain the reserved marinade into the roasting pan and boil for about 5 minutes until reduced a little. Serve separately with the wild berry sauce. The latter can be either hot or cold.

47

CURRIED LAMB WITH APRICOTS

INGREDIENTS

1 cup chopped onion
1 clove garlic, crushed
2 tbsp. butter or margarine
1 tbsp. oil
½ small green pepper, sliced
1 lb. lamb tenderloin
2 tbsp. curry powder
2 tbsp. all-purpose flour
2 cups stock, or water and bouillon cubes
1 tbsp. tomato paste
2 tbsp. superfine sugar
salt
1 cup fresh apricots, pitted

METHOD

Place the onion, garlic, butter, oil, and green pepper in a saucepan and cook to soften the onion.

Trim the lamb and cut into ½-inch pieces. Add to the pan and stir to seal the meat. Stir in the curry powder and cook for 2 minutes. Stir in the flour and gradually add the stock, tomato paste, sugar, salt, and apricots. Bring to a boil, reduce the heat, cover and simmer for 1¼ hours or until the meat is tender.

Serve with plain boiled rice, banana, chutney, and poppadums.

DUCK GALANTINE WITH ORANGE

INGREDIENTS

5½ lb. duck

1¼ lb. dark turkey meat or pork

2 tbsp. butter

1 onion, finely chopped

2 cloves garlic, crushed

1 red pepper, seeded and chopped

2 cups fresh bread crumbs

rind and juice of 2 oranges

4 sage leaves, finely chopped

4 tbsp. finely chopped parsley

salt and pepper

2 half boneless chicken breasts, skinned and cut into strips

SERVES 8~10

METHOD

Wipe the duck and place breast side down on a board. Using a small, sharp knife, cut through the skin and flesh along the backbone. Carefully ease the knife between the flesh and ribcage on one side, scraping closely to the bone until reaching the wing and leg. Repeat on the other side. Find the ball and socket joint of each leg and snip the ligaments with scissors to free the legs from the carcase. Loosen the wing joints in the same way. Cut out the bone above the wing joints, taking care to scrape away all the flesh. Continue to ease the meat away from the ribcage until it is only attached at the breastbone.

Cut against the ridge of the breastbone, taking care not to pierce the skin. Gently scrape and push the flesh off each leg bone down to the next joint, then snip the ligaments and tendons and remove the thigh bones. Leave the drumstick bones in the legs to give a good shape to the finished duck.

Prise one of the wings open and cut off the two end joints. Carefully scrape the flesh from the remaining wing joint, cut the ligaments and tendons and then pull out the bone, drawing the wing skin through to the inside. Repeat with the other wing.

Place the boned duck skin side down on a board and open it out. Retain sufficient skin to sew around the stuffing. Trim off any surplus, if necessary using scissors. Cut off the tail. Arrange the turkey or pork meat on each side of the breast.

Melt the butter and cook the onion, garlic, and pepper until soft but not browned. Stir in the bread crumbs, orange rind and juice, sage, parsley, salt and pepper. Mix well.

Place half the stuffing next to the turkey or pork on each side, then lay the chicken strips next to the stuffing, with the remaining stuffing placed in the center of the duck. Bring together to form a good duck shape and sew up from the tail to the neck end, using a trussing needle and string. Weigh and calculate the cooking time, allowing 25 minutes per 1 lb. Carefully lift on to a trivet in a roasting pan.

Preheat the oven to 350° and cook for the calculated cooking time. When cooked, stand for 10 minutes before carving, or serve cold with a seasoned orange salad.

SPICED BACON CASSEROLE

INGREDIENTS

1½ lb. diced bacon

2 tbsp. vegetable oil

1 medium-sized onion, finely chopped

2 tbsp. all-purpose flour

1¼ cups medium/dry cider

½ tsp. allspice

freshly ground pepper

1 medium-sized zucchini, sliced

1 small green eating apple, cored and sliced

1 peach, peeled and sliced

1 orange, peeled and segmented

SERVES 4~6

METHOD

Cut the bacon into bite-sized pieces. Place in a pan of cold water, bring to a boil and discard the liquid. Repeat and drain well.

Heat the oil in a large saucepan, add the onion and cook gently, without browning, until softened. Stir in the flour, gradually add the cider and bring to a boil, stirring. Add the allspice and freshly ground pepper. Cover and cook gently for 1 hour, stirring occasionally.

Add the zucchini, apple, peach and orange, and continue cooking for a further 20 minutes before serving.

BEEF CASSEROLE WITH KUMQUATS

This spicy casserole gives an interesting combination of flavors.

INGREDIENTS

1½ lb. beef stew meat

1 tbsp. all-purpose flour

salt and pepper

2 tbsp. oil

3 cups pickling onions, peeled

1 clove of garlic, crushed (optional)

14 oz. can chopped tomatoes

2 tsp. Dijon mustard

2 tbsp. chutney

1 tbsp. clear honey

1 tsp. paprika pepper

4 oz. kumquats, washed

METHOD

Preheat the oven to 325°F.

Trim the meat and cut into cubes about 1 inch thick. Place the flour in a bowl, add the seasoning and toss the meat in the flour to coat it.

Heat the oil in a flameproof casserole and cook the onions until they are lightly brown. With a slotted spoon, remove them to a plate. Add the meat and garlic to the pan and cook until lightly browned all over.

Add the tomatoes and bring to a boil. Return the onions to the pan with the remaining ingredients, add more seasoning if necessary and stir well. Cover and place in the oven and cook for 2–2½ hours until the meat is really tender.

CHAPTER
FOUR

CAKES, PUDDINGS, AND TARTS

54

BLACK CURRANT TEA BREAD
Makes 8 slices

This is an unusual way of using black currants, a rich fruit which blends well in this tea bread.

INGREDIENTS
2 cups self-rising flour

1 tsp. ground cinnamon

½ cup butter

6 tbsp. soft brown sugar

dash of salt

grated peel of 1 lemon plus 2 tbsp. juice

1 cup fresh black currants, stringed

2 eggs, beaten

4 lumps of loaf sugar, crushed

METHOD
Preheat the oven to 350°. Line a 2 lb. loaf pan with non-stick baking parchment.

Sieve the flour and cinnamon together, rub in the butter, then fold in the sugar, salt, lemon peel and juice, black currants, and eggs. Spread into the prepared cake pan, sprinkle the loaf sugar over the top and push in any visible black currants. Bake for 50–60 minutes until a skewer inserted in the center comes out clean. Leave in the pan for 5 minutes before removing to a cooling rack.

GLAZED DATE & NUT LOAF

Makes 10–12 slices

INGREDIENTS

2 cups self-rising flour

½ tsp. salt

1 tsp. ground cinnamon

1 cup soft light brown sugar

2 large eggs, beaten

½ cup soft margarine

3 cups dates, pitted and chopped

¾ cup walnuts

2 tbsp. clear honey

METHOD

Preheat the oven to 325°. Grease and line a 2 lb. loaf pan with non-stick baking parchment.

Sieve the flour, salt, and cinnamon into a mixing bowl, then add the sugar, eggs, and margarine. Beat with a wooden spoon for 2 minutes or an electric whisk for 1 minute, then fold in the dates and nuts. Place the mixture into the prepared pan, level the surface and bake for about 1¼ hours or until a skewer inserted into the center comes out clean.

Cool in the pan for 2–3 minutes then turn out onto a cooling rack. While still warm, brush the top with the honey.

ORANGE BAKEWELL TART

INGREDIENTS

½ lb. ready-made basic pie dough

3 tbsp. orange marmalade

¼ cup butter, softened

¼ cup superfine sugar

½ cup self-rising flour

¼ cup ground almonds

1 large egg

finely grated peel and juice of 1 orange

½ cup confectioners' sugar

SERVES 4–6

METHOD

Preheat the oven to 350°.

Roll out the pastry and use to line an 8 inch fluted flan pan. Spread the marmalade over the base.

Place the softened butter, superfine sugar, flour, almonds, egg, and orange peel in a bowl and beat until light and fluffy. Spread evenly in the pie shell and cook for 30–35 minutes until no mark is left when you press lightly with your fingertips. Cool before removing from the pan.

Reserving 2 tsp., sprinkle the orange juice over the tart. Mix the confectioners' sugar and remaining juice together and spread over the top of the tart. Serve either hot or cold.

MIXED FRUIT CLAFOUTIS

This is a fruit batter pudding. Any combination of fruits may be used.

INGREDIENTS

SERVES 4

1 cup all-purpose flour

dash of salt

2 eggs

1¼ cups milk

3 cups sweet cherries, pitted

1 cup fresh gooseberries, trimmed

2 tbsp superfine sugar

confectioners' sugar for dredging

METHOD

Place the flour and salt in a bowl, making a well in the center. Add the eggs and a little milk and gradually beat in a little of the flour at the same time. Continue like this, adding the milk gradually to form a thick batter and beating well to prevent lumps forming. When smooth gradually beat in the remaining milk and allow to stand for 15 minutes before using.

Meanwhile, preheat the oven to 350°. Butter and preheat a shallow ovenproof dish. Place the cherries and gooseberries in it and sprinkle with the superfine sugar. Pour over the batter and bake for 1¼ hours until the batter is risen and golden. Dredge with confectioners' sugar and serve either hot or warm with cream.

APPLE & ORANGE STRUDEL

Makes 12 slices

This is a variation on a traditional strudel using mild spicing. You can increase the spicing according to preference.

INGREDIENTS

12 oz. package frozen filo pastry (12 sheets), thawed

For the filling

1¼ lb. tart apples, peeled and diced

⅓ cup light soft brown sugar

½ cup mixed candied peel

½ tsp. mixed spice

2 tbsp. raisins

grated peel of 1 orange

2 tbsp. orange juice

6 tbsp. sweet butter, melted

¾ cup crushed Graham crackers

confectioners' sugar for dredging

METHOD

Preheat the oven to 400° and butter a large baking sheet.

Place a single layer of the filo pastry onto the baking sheet to give a square 18 × 18 inches (6 sheets) and cover with plastic wrap.

Mix the apple, sugar, peel, spice, raisins, orange peel and juice, and 1 tbsp. of the melted butter together in a large bowl.

Brush the layer of pastry with melted butter. Cover with the remaining pastry, making sure the joins are not too thick, to give an even thickness of pastry overall. Spread the filling in a single layer over the pastry, sprinkle over the crushed crackers and carefully roll up the pastry, completely enclosing the filling, to give a long roll. Seal at both ends. Finish by brushing with the remaining melted butter.

Cook for 20 minutes then reduce the oven temperature to 325° for a further 20 minutes until crisp and golden. It may be necessary to reverse the strudel during cooking depending on its position in the oven.

Transfer to a wire rack. Dredge with confectioners' sugar and serve either hot or cold.

Note: It is also possible to make this recipe with frozen puff pastry if filo pastry is not available. Roll out the pastry carefully on a lightly floured surface and stretch from underneath with your fingers to make it really thin, being careful not to pierce the pastry.

APPLE DUMPLINGS

These are everybody's favorite. The fillings can be varied using mincemeat, chopped ginger, golden raisins, corn syrup, and lemon peel – whatever takes your fancy.

INGREDIENTS

½ lb. ready-made basic pie dough

4 large tart apples

4 tsp. brown sugar

2 tbsp. raisins, chopped

finely grated peel of 1 orange

1 tbsp. superfine sugar

SERVES 4

METHOD

Preheat the oven to 400°.

Divide the pastry into 4 pieces and knead each one into a smooth round. Peel and core the apples. Place each one onto a piece of pastry. Work the pastry round the apple until almost covered. Fill the centers with brown sugar, raisins, and orange peel. Seal the pastry with a little water and stand the apples on the sealed ends in a greased baking pan. Brush over with a little water or milk and sprinkle with the superfine sugar.

Bake for 30–40 minutes, depending on the size of the apples. Serve either hot or cold, sprinkled with extra superfine sugar.

RASPBERRY & REDCURRANT MERINGUE

INGREDIENTS

For the pastry

SERVES 4~6

1 cup all-purpose flour

¼ cup plus 1 tbsp. butter, softened

2 tbsp. superfine sugar

1 small egg, beaten

For the filling

2 cups fresh raspberries

grated peel of ½ orange

2 tbsp. orange juice

2 tbsp. arrowroot flow

2 egg whites

6 tbsp. superfine sugar

1 cup fresh red currants

METHOD

Preheat the oven to 400°. Make the pastry by kneading the flour, butter, sugar, and egg together and leave on one side for 30 minutes.

Roll the pastry out on a lightly floured surface and use to line an 8 inch fluted flan pan. Prick the base, line with crumpled foil, fill with baking beans and bake blind for 15 minutes. Remove the foil and beans, reduce the oven temperature to 350° and bake for further 5–8 minutes.

Heat the raspberries and orange peel so that a little juice runs out. Blend the orange juice and arrowroot together and add to the raspberries. Cook, gently stirring, until thickened and clear. Put aside to cool.

Whisk the egg whites until stiff and dry, gradually beating in the sugar a teaspoon at a time. Fold in the red currants.

Spread the raspberry mixture into the base of the flan and completely cover with the meringue. Return to the oven for about 20 minutes until lightly browned. Serve either hot or cold.

58

BERRY CHEESECAKE

INGREDIENTS

SERVES 6~8

¼ cup butter

¼ cup plus 1 tbsp. superfine sugar

2 tsp. corn syrup

6 oz. Graham crackers, finely crushed

1 lb. tayberries, blackberries or raspberries

1 sachet gelatin dissolved in 5 tbsp. hot water

1¼ cups heavy cream

1 cup light cream cheese

6–8 tayberries, blackberries or raspberries to decorate

METHOD

Line the base of a 7 inch springclip pan with a round of wax paper.

Melt the butter, 2 tbsp. sugar and the syrup in a saucepan. Remove from the heat and stir in the cracker crumbs until evenly coated. Press the mixture evenly and firmly into the prepared pan.

Leave in a cool place to harden.

Mix half the cream with the cream cheese in a fairly large basin, until smooth. Place the berries in a saucepan with the remaining sugar and heat very gently to extract some of the juice and dissolve the sugar. Mash with a potato masher (do not use a blender as the fruit will break up too much). Stir in the dissolved gelatin to the fruit mixture and add to the cream and cream cheese mixture and pour onto the cracker base. Leave in a cold place until set.

When the cheesecake is firm loosen the sides by running a knife round, open the spring and remove to a plate. Whisk the remaining cream and use to pipe rosettes round the top edge. Decorate each rosette with the remaining berries.

BERRY ROLL

This is a light sponge made like a jelly roll and filled with cream and berries such as blackberries, raspberries or tayberries. It is ideal for freezing, but once thawed it is best eaten the same day as otherwise the sponge could become a little too soft.

INGREDIENTS

SERVES 6–8

2 eggs

¼ cup superfine sugar

½ cup all-purpose flour, sifted

extra superfine sugar for dredging

For the filling

⅔ cup heavy cream

2 cups fresh blackberries, raspberries or tayberries

confectioners' sugar for sprinkling

METHOD

Preheat the oven to 400°. Line the base and sides of a shallow 11 × 7 inch pan with wax paper and lightly brush with oil.

Place the eggs in a mixing bowl with ¼ cup superfine sugar and stand over a pan of hot water.

Whisk until the mixture is pale, fluffy and thick enough to hold the trail of the whisk. Remove the bowl from the heat and continue whisking until the mixture has cooled. Gradually fold in the flour until evenly mixed. Pour into the prepared pan and tip the pan to level the surface. Cook for 7–8 minutes.

Meanwhile, place a damp tea cloth on a working surface, cover it with a piece of wax paper larger than the pan and sprinkle with superfine sugar. When the sponge is cooked turn out immediately onto the sugared paper and carefully tear off the lining paper. Trim off the long edges of the sponge, mark off 1 inch on the short edge of the sponge and roll the sponge from here, loosely enclosing the sugared paper as you roll. Leave to become cold.

Whisk the cream until quite stiff. Carefully unroll the sponge, discard the paper, spread with the cream and berries or other fruit and carefully reroll the sponge to enclose the filling. Place on a plate and sprinkle with the confectioners' sugar.

PEACH & PASSION CAKE

This is a different version of passion cake using peaches and passion fruit, instead of bananas. This is a delicious cake to eat for dessert.

INGREDIENTS

2 cups wholewheat self-rising flour

2 tsp. baking powder

⅔ cup light soft brown sugar, sieved

2 ripe peaches, skin removed and mashed

½ cup walnuts, chopped

2 eggs, beaten

½ cup oil

1 cup fairly finely grated carrots

For the icing

6 tbsp. butter or margarine, softened

2 cups confectioners' sugar, sieved

3 passion fruit

1 peach, pitted and sliced

METHOD

Preheat the oven to 350°. Grease and line the base and sides of a 7½ inch springclip pan.

Sieve the flour and baking powder into a bowl, stir in the sugar, mashed peaches, walnuts, eggs, oil, and carrots. Place the mixture into the lined pan, spreading evenly to the sides leaving a slight hollow in the center. Bake for 50–60 minutes. Test by inserting a skewer in the center, which should come out clean. Leave to cool on a wire cooling rack.

To finish the cake, cream the butter or margarine with the confectioners' sugar until soft and fluffy. Cut the cake in half and spread the top half with some of the icing. Stir 2 passion fruit into the remaining icing and use to sandwich the two halves together.

Arrange the peach slices round the top of the cake. Fill the center with the fruit from the remaining passion fruit.

FROSTED RED CURRANT GÂTEAU

INGREDIENTS

¾ cup soft margarine

¾ cup superfine sugar

3 eggs

1½ cups self-rising flour

1 tsp. baking powder

For the filling

¼ cup softened butter or margarine

1 cup confectioners' sugar, sieved

3 cups fresh red currants, stringed

For the icing

¾ cup superfine sugar

1 egg white

2 tbsp. hot water

dash of cream of tartar

METHOD

Preheat the oven to 350°. Grease two 8 inch layer pans and line with wax paper.

Place the margarine, sugar, eggs, flour, and baking powder in a bowl and beat until pale and fluffy. Divide the mixture between the pans. Bake for 25–30 minutes until no mark is left when you lightly press it with your fingertips. Cool in the pans for 2–3 minutes before turning out onto a wire rack, removing the lining paper.

Make the filling by creaming the butter or margarine until soft and then gradually beating in the confectioners' sugar. Add half of the red currants to the filling. Stir lightly to blend and use to sandwich the two cakes together. Leave on a cooling rack placed over a plate.

Place the superfine sugar, egg white, hot water, and cream of tartar together in a bowl over a pan of hot water. Whisk until the mixture becomes thick and white and coats the back of a spoon. Remove the bowl from the heat and leave to cool, whisking from time to time. Spread the icing over the top and sides of the cake. Decorate the top with the remaining red currants. Sprinkle with a little extra confectioners' sugar.

STRAWBERRY & RASPBERRY TART

INGREDIENTS

For the pastry

1¼ cups all-purpose flour

6 tbsp. butter, softened

¼ cup superfine sugar

1 egg yolk

For the pastry cream

¼ cup cornstarch

2 cups milk

½ tsp. natural vanilla extract

¼ cup superfine sugar

2 egg yolks

For the fruit

1¾ cups strawberries

1¾ cups raspberries

4 tbsp. red currant jelly

METHOD

Place the flour, butter, sugar, and egg yolk in a bowl and knead together with the fingertips of one hand to form a dough. Leave to chill for 30 minutes.

Preheat the oven to 375°. Place an 8 inch fluted flan pan on a baking sheet.

Roll out the pastry on a lightly floured surface and use to line the flan pan, rolling off the edges. Prick the base and bake for 15–20 minutes until the pastry is golden. Remove from the oven and cool. Remove the pie shell to a serving dish.

Blend the cornstarch with a little of the milk until smooth. Heat the remaining milk with the vanilla and sugar in a saucepan until the sugar has dissolved. Pour a little of this hot milk onto the cornstarch mixture, stirring. Add this to the pan and bring to a boil. Remove from the heat. Allow to cool a little before beating in the egg yolks. Cook for 2 minutes and pour into the flan. Allow to cool.

Pick over and hull the fruit and arrange it in the flan. Melt the red currant jelly in a small saucepan with a tablespoon of water and use to brush over the fruit.

TART TATIN

This is a traditional upside-down apple pie with the fruit cooked in golden caramel.

INGREDIENTS

For the pastry

1 cup all-purpose flour

¼ cup butter

dash of superfine sugar

1 egg yolk

1 tbsp. cold water

a little lemon juice (optional)

For the caramel

½ cup granulated sugar

4 tbsp. water

For the filling

2 lb. crisp eating apples

2 tbsp. superfine sugar

METHOD

Place the flour in a bowl and rub in the butter until the mixture resembles fine crumbs. Add the superfine sugar, egg yolk, and water and use to bind the pastry, adding a little lemon juice if desired. Chill for 30 minutes.

Preheat the oven to 400°. Butter a 7 inch springclip pan.

Place the granulated sugar and water in a heavy-based saucepan. Heat gently to dissolve the sugar, shaking occasionally. Bring to a boil and cook until the caramel is golden-brown color (if it becomes too dark it will be bitter). Pour quickly into the base of the greased pan, tilting to cover the base and sides before it sets.

Peel and core the apples and cut into thin slices. Arrange the slices over the caramel, sprinkling the superfine sugar in between the slices, making sure the apples are packed firmly.

Roll out the pastry on a lightly floured surface to the same circumference as the pan. Lift carefully, using the rolling pin, and place over the apples, being careful not to stretch the pastry. If necessary, trim the edges.

Bake for 30–35 minutes until the apples are tender but still firm when tested with a skewer. Leave to cool slightly in the pan before turning out onto a heated plate. Serve hot or lukewarm with cream.

PEAR & GINGER FLAN

INGREDIENTS

For the pastry

1½ cups all-purpose flour

6 tbsp. margarine

dash of salt

2 tbsp. water

For the filling

4 ripe dessert pears

a little lemon juice

For the topping

1½ cups all-purpose flour

6 tbsp. margarine

½ cup brown sugar

¾ cup chopped candied ginger

METHOD

Make the pastry by rubbing in the flour and fat to resemble fine bread crumbs. Add the salt and water, bring the dough together with your fingertips and leave on one side for 30 minutes.

Preheat the oven to 375°.

Roll out the pastry on a lightly floured surface and use to line a 9 inch flan pan. Line with crumpled foil, fill with baking beans and bake blind for 10–15 minutes. Remove from the oven.

Peel, halve and core the pears and arrange in the pie shell. Brush with the lemon juice.

Make the topping by rubbing the flour and margarine together, then stir in the sugar and ginger. Sprinkle the topping over the pears. Bake for 30–40 minutes until the crumble has lightly browned. Serve either hot or cold.

CONTINENTAL PLUM CAKE

This is a deliciously light sponge with a difference. For best results the eggs should be weighed and the sugar, butter and flour should each be the same weight as the eggs. Take care not to let the butter overheat, becoming oily. You can use different fruit but choose firm types like apricot, mango, etc.

INGREDIENTS

SERVES 6

¾ cup superfine sugar

¾ cup butter, melted and cooled

3 eggs, separated

1½ cups self-rising flour, sieved

½ tsp. natural vanilla extract

¾ lb. firm, small plums, pitted and halved

confectioners' sugar for dredging

METHOD

Preheat the oven to 375°. Line the base of a 7½ × 10-inch roasting pan with wax paper.

Beat the superfine sugar and melted butter together until light and fluffy. Add vanilla extract and gradually beat in one egg yolk at a time. If it curdles, add a little flour.

Whisk the egg whites until stiff and gradually fold into the creamed mixture alternately with the flour. Spoon into the prepared pan, level the surface and arrange the plums over the top.

Bake for about 40–45 minutes until risen and golden and no mark is left when you press it lightly with your fingertips.

Allow to cool slightly before removing from the tin and the wax paper if serving hot. Sprinkle with confectioners' sugar and serve either hot or cold. Turn out onto a cooling rack if serving cold.

BANANA & GINGER CHEESECAKE

INGREDIENTS

6 tbsp. sweet butter

½ lb. ginger cookies, crushed

3 bananas

1 sachet gelatin dissolved in 3 tbsp. hot water

1 cup crème fraîche

⅔ cup natural yogurt

2 tbsp. clear honey

juice of ½ lemon

2 tbsp. chopped candied ginger

1 or 3 Chinese gooseberries

SERVES 6~8

METHOD

Line the base of a 7½ inch spring clip pan with wax paper.

Melt the butter in a saucepan. Add the cookies and stir until they are well coated with butter. Press the crumbs evenly into the base of the cake pan and ½ inch up the sides. Allow to set.

Mash the bananas. Mix the bananas, gelatin, crème fraîche, yogurt, honey, lemon juice, and ginger and pour onto the biscuit base. Put in a cool place to set.

Peel the Chinese gooseberries and cut into slices. Remove the cheesecake from the pan and arrange the slices around the top edge, or as shown above.

MANGO UPSIDE-DOWN PUDDING WITH MELBA SAUCE

INGREDIENTS

SERVES 4~6

1 large mango

2 tbsp. apricot jam

¾ cup butter, softened

½ cup superfine sugar

2 eggs

1 cup self-rising flour

½ tsp. natural vanilla extract

2 tbsp. milk

melba sauce (see page 102)

METHOD

Preheat the oven to 350°. Grease a 7½ inch springclip pan.

Slice the mango. Melt the jam with ¼ cup butter in a small saucepan and pour into the base of the pan. Overlap the mango slices in the base. Any mango left over may be chopped and added to the sauce.

Cream the remaining butter with the sugar until light and fluffy. Gradually beat in the eggs and fold in the flour, vanilla extract, and milk to give a soft consistency. Spoon into the pan, leveling the surface with a knife. Bake for 45–60 minutes until well risen and golden brown and no mark is left when you press it with your fingertips.

When cooked, turn out onto a warm plate and serve the melba sauce separately.

LEMON TART

INGREDIENTS

1½ cups all-purpose flour

½ cup butter

3 tbsp. superfine sugar

1 egg yolk

For the filling

grated peel and juice of 2 lemons

½ cup plus 2 tbsp. superfine sugar

3 eggs

⅔ cup heavy cream, lightly whipped

For the topping

⅔ cup water

6 tbsp. superfine sugar

1 lemon, cut into 10 slices

METHOD

Make the pastry by rubbing the flour, butter, sugar, and egg yolk together to form a dough. Cover with plastic wrap and chill for 20 minutes.

Preheat the oven to 375°.

Roll out the pastry on a lightly floured surface and use to line a deep 8 inch flan pan. Line with crumpled foil, fill with baking beans and bake blind for 10–15 minutes.

To make the filling, mix the lemon peel and juice with the sugar, eggs, and cream. Pour into the pie shell and bake for 30–40 minutes until the filling is set and the pastry is cooked. Remove and cool.

To make the topping, place the water in a small saucepan with the sugar and heat gently to dissolve. Add the lemon slices, in a single layer if possible, and cook gently until the lemon peel is soft, about 15–20 minutes. Make sure that the lemon slices are covered by the syrup.

Carefully remove the slices from the syrup with a slotted spoon and arrange on the flan – without overlapping, as this would make serving difficult. If necessary, continue cooking the syrup to reduce until really syrupy. Cool a little before pouring over the lemon slices. Serve cold with cream.

FRENCH OPEN APPLE TART

Well-flavored varieties of eating apple such as Granny Smith, Delicious or Jonathan are required for this flan.

INGREDIENTS

For the pastry

1½ cups all-purpose flour

½ cup butter

¼ cup superfine sugar

1 egg yolk

1 tsp. natural vanilla extract mixed with 1 tbsp. water

For the filling

2 lb. eating apples

1½ tbsp. lemon juice

¼ cup butter

6 tbsp. superfine sugar

METHOD

Rub the flour and butter together. Mix in the sugar with the egg yolk and vanilla and water mixture to give a fairly firm dough. Wrap in plastic wrap and

chill for 30 minutes. Roll out or press into a 10 inch flan pan.

Peel, core, quarter and slice the apples. Place in a bowl of water with 2 tsp. of the lemon juice added.

Mix the remaining lemon juice, butter, and sugar in a small pan and heat, stirring until well combined.

Preheat the oven to 400°. Line the pie shell with crumpled foil, fill with baking beans and bake blind for 10 minutes. Remove from the oven and fill with a double layer of apple slices, well packed in and overlapping neatly. Brush with the melted lemon, butter, and sugar mixture, return to the oven and cook for about 50 minutes until well browned. Brush the cooking juices over once or twice during cooking to give a good glaze and turn the flan round in the oven to give even browning. Remove from the oven and brush with the juices again. Serve either hot or cold.

BLUEBERRY TART

INGREDIENTS

2 cups all-purpose flour

¼ cup superfine sugar

¼ cup butter, softened

1 egg, lightly beaten

grated peel of 1 lemon

For the filling

1 lb. blueberries

2 tbsp. sugar

3 tbsp. cornstarch

3 tbsp. water

METHOD

Sift the flour into a mixing bowl, then add the sugar, butter, egg, and lemon peel. Mix together lightly with the fingers of one hand to make a stiff dough. Wrap in plastic wrap and chill until required.

Meanwhile, make the filling by placing the blueberries in a saucepan with the sugar. Heat gently to dissolve the sugar and slightly cook the blueberries without losing their shape. Blend the cornstarch and water together and stir into the fruit. Simmer, stirring, until thickened, then cool.

Preheat the oven to 375°. Place an 8 inch flan ring on a baking sheet.

Roll out two-thirds of the pastry on a lightly floured surface and use to line the flan ring. Fill with the cooled fruit mixture. Use the remaining pastry to make a lattice over the top. Bake for 20–25 minutes until lightly brown. Leave to cool in the flan ring. Serve cold with cream.

OTHER DESSERTS

QUICK SERVING IDEAS

FRESH FRUIT PLATTER
Choose any fruit you like, cut it into interesting shapes and sizes and arrange decoratively on individual plates garnished with a fruit leaf.

In Greece a central plate of fruit is arranged like this and guests help themselves using a fork.

FRESH FRUIT KEBABS
Arrange pieces of firm fruit, for example pear, banana, apple, strawberry, and mango, alternately on wooden skewers. Serve separately with a raspberry sauce.

FRESH FRUIT FONDUE
Put pieces of banana, pear and apple on individual plates with a fondue fork per person. In a suitable dish, melt 8 oz. chocolate with honey and nuts, add 6 tbsp. heavy cream and 2 tbsp. rum or brandy. Keep the dish warm over a bowl of hot water and place in the center of the table so that people may help themselves. (If you have one, a small fondue pot is ideal.)

PINEAPPLE WITH KIRSCH
Slice a fresh pineapple into a shallow dish and sprinkle with superfine sugar and 2–3 tbsp. of kirsch. Chill and serve. (Too much kirsch could spoil the delicate flavor of the pineapple.)

PINEAPPLE WITH STRAWBERRIES
Halve a pineapple lengthwise, scoop out the flesh, remove the core and dice the remainder. Mix in some fresh strawberries and put the mixture back into the empty shells. Purée some raspberries, sweeten with confectioners' sugar and serve spooned over the fruit.

SAUTÉED BANANAS
Melt ¼ cup butter in a skillet, add 6 tbsp. soft brown sugar and the grated peel and juice of 1 lemon and 1 orange. When the sugar has dissolved add 6 halved bananas, together with a little brandy, and cook for 5 minutes. Serve hot with ice cream.

PEARS & BANANAS WITH CHOCOLATE SAUCE
Melt 4 tbsp. corn syrup with 4 oz. dark chocolate, 2 tbsp. butter and 1 tbsp. hot water. Pour the sauce over sliced bananas and pears.

70

EXOTIC PINEAPPLE

INGREDIENTS
1 pineapple
3 tbsp. kirsch
6 oz. fresh dates, pitted and coarsely chopped
1 mango
3 passion fruit
2 small bananas
1 tbsp. shredded coconut, toasted

METHOD
Cut the top off the pineapple. Scoop out the flesh and remove the hard core. Place the pineapple flesh and kirsch in a bowl with the dates.

Slice the mango. Cut the passion fruit in half, scoop out the flesh and add with the mango to the pineapple. Slice the bananas and add with the coconut. Mix the fruits and return to the pineapple shell. If liked, serve slightly chilled with any extra fruit served separately.

GRAPE CUSTARDS

INGREDIENTS

½ lb. seedless red grapes

4 egg yolks

3 tbsp. superfine sugar

4 tbsp. marsala, madeira or sweet sherry

METHOD

Wash the grapes and place in the bottom of 4 individual glasses.

Place the egg yolks in a bowl. Beat lightly, add the sugar and wine and mix together. Place the bowl over a pan of hot water and whisk until the mixture is thick and creamy. This could take about 10 minutes.

Divide the mixture between the glasses and serve at once while still warm with sponge fingers.

BAKED STUFFED PEACHES

This popular Italian dessert may be made with fresh peaches or nectarines.

INGREDIENTS

½ cup sponge cake crumbs

¼ cup ground almonds

2 tbsp. superfine sugar

2 tbsp. dry sherry

a little butter or margarine

4 large peaches

METHOD

Preheat the oven to 350°.

Place the cake crumbs, almonds, sugar, and sherry in a bowl and mix together. Butter a shallow ovenproof dish.

Skin the peaches by dipping quickly into boiling water. Lift out with a slotted spoon and peel off the skin. Cut the peaches in half, remove the pits and fill the cavities with the almond stuffing. Place in the dish and cook for 20–30 minutes until the peaches are soft and the stuffing is lightly browned. Serve either hot or cold.

BAKED APPLE WITH LEMON

INGREDIENTS

4 large tart apples

6 tbsp. brown sugar

3 tbsp. water

grated peel of 1 lemon

⅔ cup golden raisins

½ cup Brazil nuts, chopped

METHOD

Preheat the oven to 350°.

Wipe the apples with a clean damp cloth and remove the cores. Using the point of a sharp knife, mark a line around the center through the skin. Place the apples in an ovenproof dish.

Fill the centers with half of the brown sugar. Pour the water in the dish and cook the apples for 40 minutes. Mix the lemon peel with the golden raisins and Brazil nuts. Remove the apples from the oven. Divide the filling between the apples and cook for a further 15 minutes until the apples, when tested with a skewer, are soft and cooked through. Serve hot with the juices spooned over.

JAMAICAN PUFFS

INGREDIENTS

½ lb. frozen puff pastry, thawed

4 firm bananas

lemon juice

deep oil for frying

superfine sugar

ground cinnamon, optional

METHOD

On a lightly floured surface roll out the pastry to an oblong of approximately 10 × 13 inches. Trim off the edges and cut into 8 equal lengths about 1 inch wide. Peel the bananas, cut each in half and dip in the lemon juice.

Lightly dampen each strip of pastry with a little water and wind round each piece of banana to enclose it completely, sealing the ends well.

Heat the oil and fry the bananas for 4–5 minutes until golden brown. Drain well on paper towels and roll in superfine sugar, adding a little ground cinnamon, if liked.

Serve with a little melted apricot jam.

72

APPLE & BLACKBERRY CHARLOTTE

INGREDIENTS

butter for greasing

½ lb. tart apples, sliced

6 tbsp. brown sugar

1 cup blackberries

4–6 tbsp. butter, melted

8–10 large slices bread (each about ¼ inch thick), crust removed

superfine sugar for dredging

METHOD

Grease a 4-cup soufflé dish with butter. Preheat the oven to 350°.

Cook the apples with the brown sugar until they begin to soften and then add the blackberries. Cook for 5 minutes then leave to cool.

Pour the butter into a shallow dish. Dip the slices of bread in the butter and use to line the base and sides of the dish, reserving some for the top. They should all be a tight fit.

Fill the bread case with the cooked fruit purée and use the remaining bread to completely cover the filling. Cover with wax paper or foil and bake for 40–45 minutes. Turn the charlotte out and sprinkle with superfine sugar.

FIG & PEACH SOUFFLÉ

This is a delicious, delicately flavored soufflé. The figs need to be ripe for the best flavor and the peaches not too large. Lime juice is the best to bring out the flavor, but a lemon will also bring out the flavor if limes are not available.

INGREDIENTS

½ lb. ripe figs

2 peaches

½ cup plus 2 tbsp. sugar

¼ cup water

3 eggs, separated

1 tbsp. gelatin dissolved in 5 tbsp. hot water

2 tbsp. lime or lemon juice

⅔ cup whipping cream, lightly whipped

To decorate

cream for piping

1 fig

frosted geranium leaves, if available

METHOD

Tie a double band of wax paper around a 4-cup soufflé dish. The paper should stand 2 inches above the rim of the dish and be tight against the side. Lightly brush the inside with oil.

Remove the stems from the figs, wipe the fruit and cut each into four. Skin the peaches, remove pits and cut into four.

Dissolve ¼ cup sugar in the water. Put the fruit into a pan and cook very gently to just soften the fruit. Remove, cool and blend.

Place the egg yolks in a bowl with the remaining sugar over a pan of hot water and beat until light and fluffy. Remove the pan from the heat and continue beating until cool.

Add the gelatin to the lime or lemon juice and fruit purée and add this to the egg mixture with the beaten cream.

Whisk the egg whites until stiff, fold into the fruit mixture and pour into the prepared soufflé dish. Put into a cool place until set.

Carefully remove the collar from the soufflé. Pipe cream, if liked, around the top edge and decorate with thin slices of fig and geranium leaves, if available.

ROSE MOUSSE WITH MANGOSTEEN PURÉE

This is a delicate-flavored mousse complemented by the mangosteen or rambutans. Serve in glasses accompanied with delicate cookies or sponge fingers.

INGREDIENTS

8 tbsp. rose water

1 sachet powdered gelatin

2 large eggs, separated

¼ cup superfine sugar

1 tsp. natural vanilla extract

pink food coloring

1¼ cups whipping cream

3–4 mangosteens or 6–8 rambutans

frosted rose petals, to decorate

METHOD

Pour the rose water in a small basin, sprinkle the gelatin over and leave on one side for 10 minutes for the gelatin to become spongy. Then place the basin over hot water to allow the gelatin to dissolve completely.

Put the egg yolks in a bowl with the sugar and vanilla extract, place over a pan of hot water and beat until thick and pale and the whisk leaves a trail in the mixture. Remove the bowl from the pan and continue beating until the mixture cools slightly. Stir in the gelatin and a little coloring. Whisk the cream until softly stiff and fold into the mousse mixture.

Whisk the egg whites until stiff and fold into the mousse. Add a little extra coloring if required. Spoon into 6 individual glasses and chill for several hours.

Prepare the mangosteens or rambutans, sieve them and serve separately with the mousse. Garnish each with a frosted rose petal.

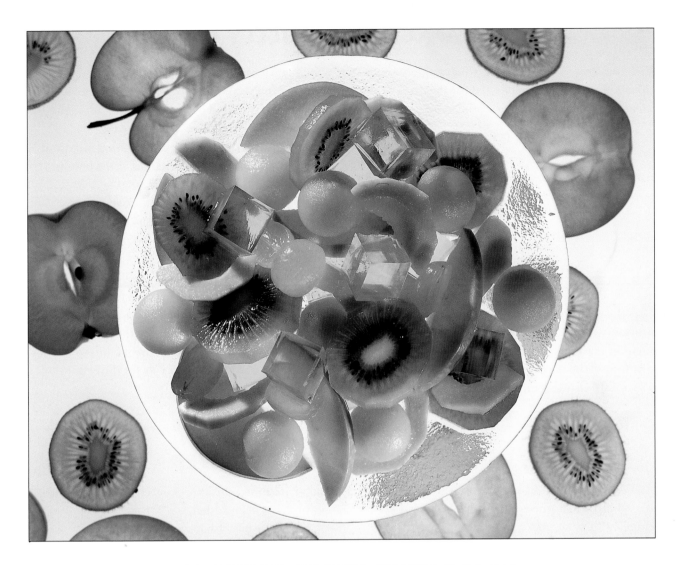

JAPANESE GREEN FRUIT SALAD

This is a refreshing salad made with exotic fruits of the same color mixed with fragrant jelly cubes of elderflower.

INGREDIENTS

For the jelly
6 leaves of gelatin
2 cups water
⅔ cup elderflower cordial
For the sugar syrup
¾ cup granulated sugar
2 cups water
For the fruit
1 small melon
3 Chinese gooseberries
1½ cups green grapes
1 green apple
2 guavas

METHOD

Soak the gelatin in half the water for 15 minutes. Add the remaining water, place in a saucepan and heat gently to dissolve. Allow to cool slightly before adding the elderflower cordial. Rinse a 7 inch shallow square pan with water and pour in the jelly mixture. Leave in a cold place to set.

To make the syrup, put the sugar and water in a saucepan and heat until the sugar has dissolved. Boil rapidly for 2–3 minutes until slightly syrupy. Remove from the heat and cool.

Cut the melon into balls or cubes and place in a large serving bowl. Peel and slice the Chinese gooseberries. Wash the grapes, halve and seed if necessary. Wash and core the apple and cut into slices. Add all these fruits to the bowl with the cooled syrup. Peel the guavas, halve and scoop out the seeds. Slice and add to the salad.

Quickly dip the pan of jelly into hot water and turn out onto damp wax paper. Cut into large cubes. Add to the salad just before serving.

CHAMPAGNE FRUIT JELLY RING

If champagne is not available, wine, apple juice, or elderflower cordial may be used for flavoring. (The sugar quantity may have to be adjusted.)

INGREDIENTS

SERVES 6

1½ oz. gelatin

1¼ cups water

¼ cup superfine sugar

1¼ cups champagne

1 cup red cherries

1¼ cups strawberries

1 cup seedless green grapes

METHOD

Soak the gelatin in half the water for approximately 5 minutes to soften. Put the remaining water and sugar in a saucepan with the champagne and heat gently until the sugar dissolves. Add the softened gelatin and also heat until dissolved, without boiling. Allow to cool.

Wash, halve and pit the cherries. Hull and wash the strawberries and halve if necessary. Wash the grapes.

Pour a layer of the jelly in a 4-cup ring mold and allow to set. Place a ring of cherries in the base and pour over a little jelly and allow to set.

Arrange the remaining fruit in layers, setting with a little jelly each time, until all have been used. Pour over any remaining jelly and put into a cool place until firm.

To turn out, dip quickly in hand-hot water to loosen the jelly, put a plate over the top and invert.

Note: Care should be taken not to leave the jelly in the water too long as it will melt the jelly and spoil the effect. Any combination of fruits would be suitable but always use clear jelly for the best appearance.

EXOTIC MERINGUE FLOWER

Any selection of fruits may be used for this recipe. It's an attractive presentation that will stun everybody!

INGREDIENTS

SERVES 4~6

3 egg whites

¾ cup superfine sugar

⅔ cup heavy cream

1 cup each of 5 fresh fruits e.g. mango, Chinese gooseberries, mangosteen, passion fruit, and banana

METHOD

Preheat the oven to 225°. Place a sheet of vegetable parchment on a baking sheet and draw a 7½ inch circle.

Place the egg whites in a mixing bowl and whisk until stiff and dry. Gradually fold in a teaspoon of sugar at a time, whisking between each spoonful, until all has been added.

Fit a large pastry bag with a large fluted vegetable tip. Fill the bag with most of the meringue and spread the remaining meringue in a circle on the parchment. Pipe petal shapes, forming 5 individual cases of meringue on top of the circle. Then pipe a second row on top of the first petal shapes to make the cases deeper.

Place in the oven for at least 3 hours until crisp and dry. Remove from oven and allow to cool before removing the paper.

Put the meringues carefully on a plate. Lightly whisk the cream and spread in the base of each case. Prepare the fruits, slice if necessary and arrange a different fruit in each petal to give a colorful presentation.

FRESH PEACH MELBA

INGREDIENTS

SERVES 4

4 peaches

vanilla ice cream

melba sauce (double quantity, see page 102)

METHOD

Skin, halve and pit the peaches. Place in 4 individual sundae glasses with ice cream scoops and serve with the melba sauce poured over. Serve at once with wafers.

FRESH FRUIT BRÛLÉE

INGREDIENTS

1¼ cups fresh raspberries

1¼ cups fresh strawberries, sliced

1 cup fresh red currants, stringed

1¼ cups heavy cream

1 cup brown sugar, approximately

SERVES 4–6

METHOD

Place the fruit in either a flameproof dish or 4–6 individual flameproof dishes.

Whip the cream until fairly thick and use to cover the fruit evenly. Sprinkle over the brown sugar to completely hide the cream and chill well.

Just before serving, place the dish or dishes under a preheated broiler to lightly melt and caramelize the sugar.

Serve immediately.

ORANGE & STRAWBERRY SYLLABUB

No cookery book would be complete without a syllabub; try this fruit version. The fruits may be varied, depending on the time of year.

INGREDIENTS

1¼ cups fresh strawberries
juice and coarsely grated peel of 1 orange
1 tbsp. Grand Marnier or Cointreau
3 tbsp. superfine sugar
⅔ cup white wine
1 tsp. lemon juice
1¼ cups heavy cream
2 egg whites

SERVES 6

METHOD

Wash and hull the strawberries. Slice and arrange in the bottom of 6 sundae glasses. Sprinkle the orange juice and the liqueur over the strawberries.

Place the superfine sugar, wine, and lemon juice in a mixing bowl. Add half the grated orange peel together with the cream and stir until the ingredients are absorbed by the cream.

Whisk the egg whites until stiff. Add to the cream and continue whisking until the mixture is softly stiff. Spoon on top of the strawberries and sprinkle with the remaining orange peel. Serve well chilled.

BAKED BANANAS WITH MANGO

INGREDIENTS

SERVES 4

4 medium-sized bananas
2 small mangoes
2 tbsp. lemon juice
1 lime

METHOD

Preheat the oven to 400°. Place the unpeeled bananas on a baking sheet and cook for 10 minutes until the skins have blackened.

Meanwhile, cut the mangoes in half each side of the pit and cut into wedges, removing the peel if preferred.

Remove the bananas from the oven, cut a sliver of skin from the base of each banana so that they sit upright, make 2 parallel cuts along the top of each, then cut away the center section of skin. Sprinkle the banana flesh with lemon juice.

Place the bananas in serving dishes and arrange the mango wedges along the top. Cut the lime into slices, halve each slice and arrange alternately between the mango wedges.

Serve with cream, sprinkled with dark brown sugar.

78

FRUIT CHOW-CHOW

INGREDIENTS

1 small ripe papaya

1 mango

4 passion fruit

4 apple bananas

2 Chinese gooseberries

½ lb. lychees, lungan or rambutan

1 large, ripe custard apple

METHOD

Prepare the papaya and mango and slice into a bowl. Halve the passion fruit and scoop out the flesh into the bowl. Peel the bananas and Chinese gooseberries, slice and add. Remove the skin and pits from the lychee, lungan or rambutan and add.

Open the custard apple and remove the fruit. Place into a nylon sieve and press out the juice over the other fruits. Stir round gently and serve at once.

CRISPY PEARS

INGREDIENTS

3 tbsp. butter or margarine

1 ½ cups fresh bread crumbs

3 tbsp. brown sugar

1 lb. fresh pears

1 tbsp. lemon juice

METHOD

Preheat the oven to 375°.

Melt the butter or margarine in a pan. Add the bread crumbs and cook, stirring, until the butter has been absorbed and the crumbs are beginning to brown. Stir in the sugar and cook for a few seconds. Allow to cool.

Peel and core the pears, cut into slices and place in a small pie dish. Sprinkle with the lemon juice and spoon over the cooled crumb mixture. Cook for 20–25 minutes. Serve hot.

APRICOT RATAFIA JELLY

The combination of apricot and ratafia is so good and unusual, and the jelly on a crisp base complements this dish perfectly.

INGREDIENTS

2 tbsp. superfine sugar

⅔ cup water

1 lb. fresh apricots, pits removed

1 sachet powered gelatin dissolved in 5 tbsp. hot water

¼ cup sweet butter

¾ cup ratafias, crushed

¾ cup plain cookies, crushed

⅔ cup heavy cream (optional)

extra ratafias, to decorate

METHOD

Dissolve the sugar in the water and gently poach the pitted apricots until just soft but still retaining their shape. Gently stir in the dissolved gelatin and pour this mixture into a 4-cup soufflé dish. Put in a cold place until set.

Melt the butter in a saucepan, remove from the heat and stir in the crushed ratafias and cookies. Stir until well coated in the butter. Spread this mixture evenly on top of the set jelly, pressing it to make a firm base. Leave to become cold.

Ease a knife very carefully round the edge of the cookies, then quickly dip the dish in hot water. Place a plate on top, quickly invert the dish and shake out the jelly onto the plate. If liked, pipe rosettes of cream round the top edge and decorate with extra ratafias.

GOLDEN SUMMER PUDDING

This dish requires a total of 2 lb. fruit.

INGREDIENTS

SERVES
6

2 oranges

2 cups water

6 tbsp. granulated sugar

2 peaches or 1 nectarine

2 mangoes

10–12 slices white bread

To decorate

slices of mango (optional)

slices of orange (optional)

METHOD

Remove the peel from the oranges and place in a saucepan with the water and sugar. Dissolve the sugar and cook gently for 2 minutes to extract the flavor from the orange peel. Remove the pan from the heat and discard the orange peel.

Skin the peaches and mangoes and remove the pits. Cut the flesh into small dice, add to the flavored syrup and cook to just soften the fruit, about 5 minutes. Remove from the heat.

Cut 12 rounds of bread to fit the base and tops of six ⅔ cup ramekin dishes and place a round in the base of each dish. Cut small squares of bread and use to line the sides of the dishes.

Using a slotted spoon, fill each dish with the fruit, reserving the syrup to serve with the puddings. Top each with the remaining circles of bread, pressing down well. Cover each tightly with plastic wrap and leave to chill overnight.

To serve, remove carefully from the dishes, spoon the remaining syrup over and decorate, if liked, with extra slices of mango or orange.

CHAPTER SIX

FROSTY FRUITS

SATSUMA & GINGER SHERBET

GRAPEFRUIT ICE CREAM

SURPRISE BANANA PUFFS

**GOOSEBERRY &
ELDERFLOWER SHERBET**

WATERMELON GRANITA

**PEACH SWIRLS WITH
ORANGE CARAMEL SAUCE**

ICED BLACK CURRANT SOUFFLÉ

LYCHEE & LIME SHERBET

PAPAYA & LIME ICE CREAM

**TOMATO, ORANGE, &
BASIL SHERBET**

**REAL RASPBERRY RIPPLE
ICE CREAM**

SATSUMA & GINGER SHERBET

SERVES 8

INGREDIENTS

8 large satsumas

½ inch piece fresh ginger, peeled and grated

¾ cup superfine sugar

finely grated peel and juice of 1 lemon

finely grated peel and juice of 1 small orange

finely grated peel and juice of ½ grapefruit

1 egg white

METHOD

Cut the tops off the satsumas and reserve. Using a grapefruit knife, cut out the fruit. Place the empty shells in tartlet pans. Remove the seeds from the fruit and blend the pulp with the ginger. Strain into a saucepan, add the sugar and heat until dissolved. Add the grated peel and juice of the lemon, orange, and grapefruit. Put into a suitable container for the freezer and freeze until just firm. Remove from the freezer and beat.

Whisk the egg white until stiff and fold into the frozen mixture. Spoon into the empty shells, top each with the reserved lids, return these to the tartlet pans and freeze until firm.

GRAPEFRUIT ICE CREAM

INGREDIENTS

3 ruby grapefruit

1½ cups confectioners' sugar

1¼ cups heavy cream, whipped

6 frosted lemon geranium leaves, to decorate (optional)

METHOD

Cut the grapefruit in half and carefully squeeze out the juice. Reserve the shells and freeze. The juice should measure 1 cup. Strain into a bowl and mix in the sugar until dissolved.

Fold the juice into the whipped cream, place in a suitable container and freeze, beating twice when the mixture starts to freeze. After the second beating, spoon into the grapefruit halves and freeze until solid.

Remove from the freezer 30 minutes before serving and decorate, if liked, with a frosted lemon geranium leaf.

Note: To frost lemon geranium leaves, brush clean leaves with a little egg white and dip into superfine sugar. Put in a warm place to dry, when they are ready to use. They keep well.

SURPRISE BANANA PUFFS

Makes approximately 20 puffs

INGREDIENTS

1 lb. ripe bananas

juice of 1 orange

⅓ cup light soft brown sugar

1 cup Greek yogurt

For the choux pastry

¼ cup butter or margarine

½ cup water

½ cup plus 2 tbsp. all-purpose flour

2 eggs

For the caramel sauce

1 cup sugar

8 tbsp. water

METHOD

Peel and mash the bananas in a bowl with the orange juice and sugar. Whisk in the yogurt, pour into a suitable container and freeze, beating 3 times at regular intervals.

Place the butter or margarine in a medium-sized saucepan and pour in the water. Heat gently until the fat melts, then turn the heat up and bring to a full boil. Tip in all the flour, remove the pan from the heat and mix until smooth, when it should come away from the sides of the pan. Allow to cool.

Preheat the oven to 425°. Grease 2 baking sheets. Have ready a large pastry bag fitted with a large fluted vegetable tip.

Beat the eggs and gradually beat into the lukewarm mixture in the pan. Continue beating until the mixture is smooth and glossy.

Fill the pastry bag with the mixture and pipe small mounds on to the greased baking sheets, leaving enough space between for the mixture to rise. Bake for 10 minutes, then reduce the oven temperature to 375° and cook for a further 10 minutes. Remove from the oven. Slit and cool on a wire rack.

Make the caramel by placing the sugar and remaining water in a saucepan. Heat gently to dissolve the sugar. When dissolved, bring to a boil and cook until it begins to change color. (Take great care not to get splashed with the boiling liquid.) When the syrup becomes a golden color, cover your hand with a tea-cloth, lift the pan from the heat and quickly dip the base in cold water to stop the caramel overcooking. Add a little boiling water to the pan for a runny caramel for pouring over the puffs. Keep on one side.

Place the ice cream in the refrigerator for 30 minutes before filling the puffs. Serve with the caramel sauce.

Note: These can be filled in advance and returned to freezer until ready for serving, but they do need to be in a refrigerator for 30 minutes before serving.

GOOSEBERRY & ELDERFLOWER SHERBET

INGREDIENTS

1 lb. gooseberries, trimmed

¾ cup sugar

juice of ½ lime

½ cup water

⅓ cup elderflower cordial

green coloring (optional)

SERVES 4

METHOD

Place the gooseberries in a saucepan with the sugar, lime juice, water, and elderflower cordial. Cook gently until soft.

Purée the fruit and pass through a fine sieve. Add a little green coloring, if liked.

Allow to cool before placing in a suitable container. Cover and freeze, beating 3 times at intervals.

Place in the refrigerator 30 minutes before serving.

WATERMELON GRANITA

INGREDIENTS

1 medium-sized watermelon

½ cup confectioners' sugar

⅔ cup ginger ale

1 tbsp. lemon or lime juice

SERVES 8

METHOD

Cut into the top of the watermelon in a zig-zag pattern, then lift the top off carefully.

Using a spoon, scoop out the flesh and remove all the seeds. Freeze the shell. Place the flesh in a blender in batches and blend until smooth. Pour into a bowl.

Dissolve the confectioners' sugar in the ginger ale, stir in the lemon or lime juice and add to the melon. Pour into a suitable container. Freeze until ice crystals form around the edges, then draw these into the mixture. Freeze until the whole is a mass of small crystals. Spoon into the reserved shell and serve.

PEACH SWIRLS WITH ORANGE CARAMEL SAUCE

INGREDIENTS

3 medium-sized ripe peaches

1½ tsp. gelatin dissolved in 2 tbsp. hot water

⅔ cup heavy cream, whipped

1 egg white

½ cup confectioners' sugar, sieved

extra peach slices, to decorate

For the Caramel

SERVES 4–6

½ cup superfine sugar

⅓ cup water

¼ cup boiling water

grated peel and juice of ½ orange

METHOD

Purée and sieve the peaches to remove any stringy pieces. Add the gelatin to the purée. When almost set stir in the whipped cream. Whisk the egg white and fold in the confectioners' sugar and chill.

Line 2 baking sheets with plastic wrap and pipe about 20 swirls onto the sheets. Freeze until solid.

To make the caramel, in a medium-sized saucepan dissolve the sugar in the water and boil until a dark golden caramel color. Cover your hand holding the pan with a tea-cloth and, taking care, add the boiling water. Remove the pan from the heat when this has combined and add the orange peel and juice.

Serve the swirls with a little sauce poured over and, if liked, decorate with extra peach slices.

ICED BLACK CURRANT SOUFFLE

INGREDIENTS

3 cups black currants, stringed

¾ cup sugar

2 egg whites

½ cup confectioners' sugar, sieved

1¼ cups whipping cream

SERVES 6

METHOD

Wrap a double thickness of foil round a 4-cup soufflé dish to extend 2 inches above the rim of the dish.

Cook the black currants with the sugar until soft, purée in a blender then strain. Allow to cool.

Whisk the egg whites until stiff then gradually whisk in the confectioners' sugar.

Whip the cream until softly stiff. Place the fruit purée in a large bowl and gradually fold in the egg white and cream. Pour into the prepared soufflé dish, level the surface and freeze for several hours until solid. Remove the foil and serve.

LYCHEE & LIME SHERBET

INGREDIENTS

SERVES 4

1 lb. fresh lychees

juice of 1 lime

¾ cup confectioners' sugar, sieved

1 egg white

METHOD

Peel the lychees and remove the pits. Place the flesh in a blender with the lime juice and confectioners' sugar. Process until smooth.

Pour into a container suitable for the freezer, freeze until slushy, then beat well. Repeat this twice.

Whisk the egg white until firm and fold into the sherbet. Freeze for several hours until solid.

Serve in small scoops with slices of fresh mango or other suitable exotic fruit, or with another fruit sherbet – mango, Chinese gooseberry, etc.

PAPAYA & LIME ICE CREAM

INGREDIENTS

2 medium-sized papayas (about 1¼ lb.)

juice of 2 limes

2 tbsp. fresh orange juice

1½ cups confectioners' sugar

1¼ cups heavy cream, whipped

SERVES 6

METHOD

Peel the papayas, halve, and remove the seeds. Purée the flesh and mix with the juices and sugar.

Fold in the whipped cream and pour into a suitable container. Freeze until firm, beating twice at intervals.

Put in the refrigerator 30 minutes before serving.

If liked, serve with extra pieces of papaya and a crisp cookie.

TOMATO, ORANGE, & BASIL SHERBET

INGREDIENTS

4¼ cups tomato juice

juice of ½ lemon

1 tbsp. Worcestershire sauce

2 tsp. finely chopped basil

finely grated peel and juice of 1 orange

2 drops hot pepper sauce

salt and pepper

2 egg whites

basil leaves, to garnish

METHOD

Mix together the tomato juice, lemon juice, Worcestershire sauce, basil, orange peel and juice, and hot pepper sauce. Season with salt and pepper to taste. Pour into a suitable container and freeze for 1½ hours until mushy.

Remove from the freezer and whisk well, then return to the freezer for a further 1 hour until it is again mushy. Whisk once more.

Whisk the egg whites until stiff and fold into the tomato mixture. Return to the freezer and freeze until solid.

Put in the refrigerator 30 minutes before serving. Spoon into individual dishes and garnish with basil leaves. Serve with Melba toast.

REAL RASPBERRY RIPPLE ICE CREAM

Makes approximately 4 cups

INGREDIENTS

½ cup all-purpose flour

4 egg yolks

6 tbsp. superfine sugar

2 tsp. natural vanilla extract

2½ cups milk

1¼ cups whipping cream

1¾ cups fresh raspberries, sieved

2 tbsp. confectioners' sugar, sieved

METHOD

Place the flour in a basin with the egg yolks, sugar, and vanilla and stir in sufficient milk to give a thin, smooth paste. Heat the remaining milk in a saucepan, bring just to a boil and stir slowly into the blended mixture, making sure there are no lumps.

Return to the pan and bring slowly to a boil, stirring. It will become quite thick and it is necessary to beat well to prevent any lumps forming. Reduce the heat and cook for 3–4 minutes – the custard should just bubble. Remove the pan from the heat, cover with a piece of damp wax paper and allow to become cold.

Whisk the cream until softly stiff, beat the custard and fold in the cream. Place the mixture in a suitable container and freeze for 3–4 hours until it is partly frozen.

Mix the raspberries and confectioners' sugar together. Remove the ice cream from the freezer, beat well and swirl in the raspberry mixture. Return to the freezer until solid.

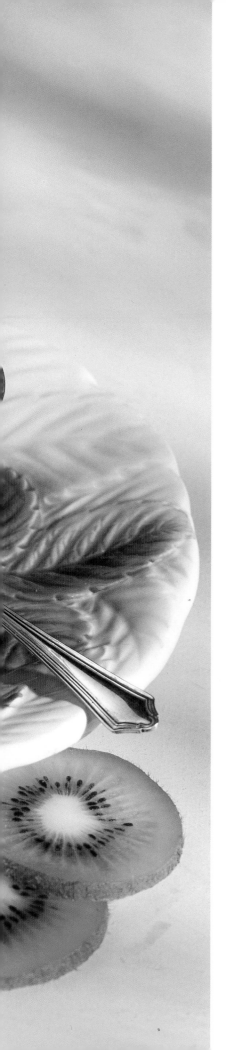

SAUCES, DRESSINGS, AND RELISHES

FLAVORED OILS

Flavored oils can be made with herbs. Use a light oil. Thoroughly wash and dry fresh, young herbs and place them in a clean jar or bottle with an air-tight lid. Pour in the oil, cover and leave for at least 1 month to mature.

Fruit oils can also be made this way. Thoroughly wash lemons and oranges, thinly pare the peel and place in jars as above. Cover and leave for at least 1 month to mature.

These oils can be used as a change from traditional oils.

ORANGE DRESSING

Makes ½ cup

INGREDIENTS

dash each of salt and pepper

½ tsp. Dijon mustard

4 tbsp. orange oil

1 tbsp. orange juice

1 tbsp. cider vinegar

1 tsp. sugar

METHOD

Place the seasonings and mustard in a small bowl, gradually blend in the orange oil to make an emulsion and mix in the remaining ingredients. Taste and adjust the seasoning, if necessary, and use as required.

BANANA RELISH

Makes ¾ cup

Serve this relish with pork, ham, bacon, and barbecued food.

INGREDIENTS

1 tbsp. butter

1 small onion, finely chopped

2 tsp. wholegrain mustard

1 tsp. sugar

4 medium-sized bananas, peeled

2 tsp. white malt vinegar

1 tsp. Worcestershire sauce

METHOD

Melt the butter and fry the onion slowly, without browning, until soft. Stir in the mustard and sugar and cook for 1 minute.

Mash the bananas and add the remaining ingredients. Cook for 2–3 minutes to soften the banana.

VINAIGRETTE DRESSING

Makes 1¼ cups

There is such a wide choice of oils, vinegars, and mustards available that you can make a vinaigrette dressing very much to your own taste. This is a basic recipe that can be altered according to preference and the type of dish for which it is required. This quantity can be made in advance and stored.

INGREDIENTS

4 tbsp. vinegar

dash each of dry mustard, salt, and freshly ground pepper

1 tsp. superfine sugar

1 cup oil

METHOD

Mix the vinegar with the seasonings and sugar. Gradually add the oil, beating well until the dressing thickens.

FIVE CITRUS SAUCE

Makes 1¼ cups

A sauce with a difference that is ideal to serve with rich meats such as duck, goose, and pork. Any combination of citrus fruits could be used.

INGREDIENTS

1 pink grapefruit

1 ordinary grapefruit

2 honey tangerines

1 orange

1 lime

2 minneolas

4 inch piece of leek, finely sliced

2 tbsp. butter

2 tbsp. sugar

2 tbsp. cornstarch

METHOD

Using a sharp knife, cut off the peel and pith from the pink grapefruit and cut out the segments. Keep on one side. Squeeze the juice from the second grapefruit.

Prepare the honey tangerines in the same way as the grapefruit. Thinly peel the peel from the orange and lime and cut this into very thin shreds. Place these shreds in a pan of cold water. Bring slowly to a boil and cook until they are just softened. Drain and rinse in cold water.

Squeeze the juice from the orange, lime, and 1 minneola. Measure the juices to make up to 1¼ cups. Segment the second minneola.

Using a small saucepan, cook the leek in the butter gently, without browning, until soft. Stir in the sugar and cook for a few seconds. Blend the cornstarch with a little of the fruit juice, add to the pan with the remaining juice and cook for about 2 minutes until thickened and clear. Stir in the fruit segments and the shredded peel. Heat gently and serve either hot or cold.

BLACKBERRY CATSUP

Makes 4 cups

This is a fairly sharp, fruity sauce to serve with sausages, pork chops, duck, and turkey. It is also an ideal accompaniment to barbecued food. A combination of blackberries and elderberries or black currants and apple could be used instead.

INGREDIENTS

2 lb. blackberries

3 cups chopped onions

1¼ cups white malt vinegar

¼ tsp. ground cloves

½ tsp. ground allspice

½ tsp. turmeric

1⅓ cups light soft brown sugar

METHOD

Pick over the blackberries and wash them. Place the onions in a fairly large saucepan with the vinegar and cook for 5 minutes. Add the remaining ingredients and cook for 30 minutes. Allow to cool slightly before blending. Sieve the purée to remove all seeds. Pour into sterilized bottles.

LEMON FENNEL SAUCE
Makes 1¼ cups

This is a sharp, tangy, pouring sauce.

INGREDIENTS

3 tbsp. butter

1 bulb fresh fennel, finely chopped

2 tsp. flour

grated peel of 1 lemon

juice of 2 lemons

⅔ cup water

1 tbsp. fresh fennel leaves, chopped

1 tsp. sugar

salt and freshly ground white pepper

METHOD

Melt the butter in a saucepan, add the chopped fennel and stir. Cover and cook gently for 5 minutes to soften.

Add the flour and cook for 30 seconds, then stir in the lemon peel and juice, together with the water. Bring to a boil and cook for a further 2 minutes until thickened. Add the fennel leaves and sugar, if required. Season to taste.

PLUM & CLARET SAUCE

Serve this sauce with ice cream or cheesecake.

INGREDIENTS

½ lb. red plums

⅞ cup plus 2 tbsp. water

½ cup plus 2 tbsp. sugar

½ cup claret

2 tsp. arrowroot flour

2 tbsp. water

SERVES 4

METHOD

Wash the plums, halve them and remove the pits. Place the plums, ⅞ cup water and sugar in a saucepan, heat and stir to dissolve the sugar. Add the claret and cook until the plums are soft. Sieve or blend the plums and return to the saucepan.

Blend the arrowroot with 2 tbsp. water and stir into the purée. Bring to a boil, stirring, until thickened and clear. If the sauce appears too thick, add a little extra water or orange juice.

SAVORY KUMQUAT SAUCE
Makes 2½ cups

This is a savory, orange-type sauce to serve with duck, pork, turkey, or liver.

INGREDIENTS

2 scallions or green onions, trimmed and sliced

1 tsp. freshly grated ginger

peel of 1 lime, thinly cut into strips

½ cup kumquats, cut into quarters with seeds removed

½ chicken bouillon cube

2½ cups water

finely grated peel and juice of 1 orange

3 tbsp. cornstarch

2 tbsp. sugar

METHOD

Put the onions, ginger, lime, kumquats, bouillon cube, and water into a saucepan and cook for about 10–15 minutes until the kumquats are soft. Blend the orange juice and peel with the cornstarch and stir into the kumquat mixture. Bring slowly to a boil, stirring, and cook for 2–3 minutes until thickened and clear. Add sugar to taste.

FRUITY BARBECUE SAUCE
Makes 2 cups

INGREDIENTS

2 tbsp. vegetable oil

1 onion, chopped

2 x 14 oz. cans chopped tomatoes

3 cloves garlic, crushed

⅓ cup brown sugar

4 tbsp. malt vinegar

2 tbsp. Worcestershire sauce

1 tbsp. tomato paste

2 peaches, 1 banana

4 slices fresh pineapple

METHOD

Place the oil in a saucepan with the onion, tomatoes, garlic, brown sugar, vinegar, Worcestershire sauce, and tomato paste. Simmer for 15 minutes until the sauce has thickened.

Meanwhile, peel the peaches, remove the pits and chop the flesh. Peel and slice the banana and chop the pineapple. Add these to the sauce and cook slowly for 5 minutes to soften the fruit without losing its shape.

STRAWBERRY & CHINESE GOOSEBERRY RELISH
Makes 1¼ cups

This recipe could be made with thick cream, crème fraîche or Greek yogurt instead of mayonnaise, depending on the accompanying dishes and personal preference. Serve this relish chilled with a collation of cold meats.

INGREDIENTS
dash each of salt and freshly ground white pepper
1 tsp. sugar
½ tsp. Dijon mustard
2 tbsp. light oil
1 tbsp. tarragon vinegar
3 tbsp. mayonnaise
2 tsp. chopped fresh tarragon
1¾ cups strawberries, sliced
1 Chinese gooseberry, peeled, sliced and quartered

METHOD
Place the seasoning, sugar, and mustard in a bowl, stir in the oil and gradually beat in the vinegar, mayonnaise, and tarragon. Add the strawberries and the Chinese gooseberry.

FRUIT COULIS

These consist of puréed soft fruits strained of seeds and skin and are of a pouring consistency. They are used to pour over ice cream, fruit terrines, pavlova, creams, cheesecakes, summer puddings, and many other dishes.

MELBA SAUCE

Makes 1¼ cups

INGREDIENTS

1 lb. fresh raspberries

8 tbsp. confectioners' sugar, sifted

METHOD

Pick over the fresh raspberries, rub through a nylon strainer into a bowl and gradually beat in the confectioners' sugar, 1 tablespoon at a time.

FRUIT KISSELS

This is a mixture of cooked berries thickened with cornstarch, arrowroot flour, potato flour or gelatin and served chilled with thick cream.

CELERY & APRICOT SAUCE

Serve this sauce with pork, lamb, duck, or fried crumbed mackerel. Plums or gooseberries would also make a good savory, fruity sauce.

SERVES 4

INGREDIENTS

3 tbsp. butter

½ cup chopped onion

1 stalk celery, finely sliced

3 cups fresh apricots, pitted

salt and pepper

2 tsp. freshly chopped parsley

sugar to taste

METHOD

Melt the butter, add the onion and celery and cook slowly until soft but not browned – about 5 minutes.

Cut the apricots into quarters and add to the onion mixture with salt and pepper to taste. Cook just to soften the fruit and reduce any liquid. Stir in parsley and add sugar to taste.

CHERRY & ORANGE SAUCE

Makes 2½ cups

This is a savory sauce to serve with duck, pork, and venison.

INGREDIENTS

¼ cup finely chopped onion

2 cups fresh cherries, pitted

½ chicken bouillon cube

2 cups water

¼ cup port or cherry brandy

¼ cup cornstarch

finely grated peel and juice of 1 orange

1 tbsp. red wine vinegar

freshly ground pepper to taste

METHOD

Place the onion and the cherries in a saucepan with the bouillon cube dissolved in the water. Cook for 5 minutes to soften the onion and cherries.

Blend the port or cherry brandy with the cornstarch and add to the saucepan with the remaining ingredients. Heat gently, stirring continuously. Bring to a boil and cook for 2–3 minutes until the sauce is thickened and clear.

Taste and adjust the seasoning if necessary.

APPLE & MINT SAUCE

SERVES
6

INGREDIENTS

2 tbsp. butter or margarine

1 cup sliced onions

½ lb. tart apples, peeled and sliced

2 tbsp. granulated sugar

2 tbsp. chopped fresh mint

salt and pepper

METHOD

Melt the butter, add the onions and cook gently for 5 minutes without browning.

Add the apples, cover and simmer gently for 5 minutes until just beginning to break up. Stir in the remaining ingredients.

Serve hot or cold with roast or broiled lamb.

POTS OF FRUIT

FLAVORED VINEGARS

BEET & ORANGE CHUTNEY

FRUIT & NUT PICKLE

TROPICAL JAM

MANGO & GREEN TOMATO
CHUTNEY

GOOSEBERRY & GARLIC
CHUTNEY

MANGO CHUTNEY

HOT LIME PICKLE

PINEAPPLE PICKLE

PAPAYA & ORANGE PICKLE

PLUM & PUMPKIN PICKLE

RED CURRANT & APPLE PICKLE

SWEET PLUM CHUTNEY

QUINCE JELLY

SPICED PICKLED PEARS

DAMSON CHEESE

SEVILLE ORANGE MARMALADE

RED CURRANT & ORANGE JELLY

STRAWBERRY &
GOOSEBERRY JAM

FLAVORED VINEGARS

Flavored vinegars are often required in cookery and are popular, very easy to make and much cheaper than commercially prepared types.

It is necessary to use good quality vinegars. Cider and wine vinegars are more costly, but well worth the extra expense. They do have a stronger flavor but they are a good base to use with highly flavored additions, for example hot spices.

Vinegars flavored with herbs and fruit are excellent for making salad dressings and sauces. They may also be used in pickling eggs, new potatoes, onions, beet and fruits such as plums, apricots, apples, and pears.

FRUIT VINEGARS

Use equal quantities of soft fruit to a good vinegar. [See also recipe for Raspberry Vinegar]

GARLIC VINEGAR

This recipe doesn't use fruit, but makes a great vinegar.

INGREDIENTS
Use 1 bulb of garlic to 2½ cups vinegar

METHOD
Peel and chop the garlic, add to the vinegar and bring slowly to a boil. Pour into a bowl, cover and leave for 1 week. Strain and bottle.

HERB VINEGARS

The stronger herbs lend themselves to flavoring vinegar very well. If you use a mixture of herbs, make sure the balance is right so that they complement each other.

If you have available a big selection of fresh herbs, it is easy to make a few bottles of each at any one time when the herbs are at their best.

INGREDIENTS
3 oz. fresh herb
2½ cups vinegar

METHOD
Wash the herb, dry it and place it in a large saucepan with the vinegar. Bring slowly to a boil. Transfer to a bowl and squeeze the herb with a metal spoon against the side of the bowl. Cover with vinegar and leave to stand for 2–3 weeks, stirring each day. Strain through a fine sieve into bottles, adding a sprig of the appropriate herb to each. Cover with screw tops.

RASPBERRY VINEGAR

Makes 3¾ cups

INGREDIENTS

1 lb. raspberries

2½ cups cider vinegar

½ cup superfine sugar

METHOD

Mash the fruit with the vinegar and sugar. Cover and leave for 2 days. Strain through cheesecloth or fine cotton and pour into bottles. This is the best straining but there can still be more juice and vinegar to be squeezed from the cheesecloth. This will be cloudy, so keep it in a separate jar.

CITRUS VINEGAR

METHOD

Use 3 oranges or lemons to each 2½ cups of wine vinegar. Peel the peel from the fruit and chop finely. Place in a large saucepan, squeeze the juice and add with the vinegar. Bring the mixture slowly to boiling point, pour into large bowl and leave for 2 weeks. Strain through a fine sieve into bottles. Add a thin strip of orange or lemon peel to each bottle and cover with a screw top.

BEET & ORANGE CHUTNEY

Makes approximately 5 lb.

INGREDIENTS

1 lb. tart apples

1 lb. onions

2 tbsp. horseradish sauce

2 tsp. salt

pepper

¼ tsp. ground cloves

2½ cups malt vinegar

1 lb. granulated sugar

2 lb. cooked beet

grated peel of 2 oranges

METHOD

Peel, core and chop the apples. Peel and chop the onions. Put into a pan with the horseradish sauce, salt, pepper, cloves, vinegar, and sugar. Heat gently and stir occasionally until the sugar dissolves. Simmer for 20 minutes.

Meanwhile, peel and chop the beet. Segment the oranges. Add to the pan and continue simmering for 15–20 minutes.

Put the hot chutney into warmed jars. Cover with acid-resistant tops when cold.

FRUIT & NUT PICKLE

Makes approximately 2¾ lb.

This pickle has a unique texture because of the different types of fruit, which should be kept as whole as possible. The fruits can be varied but mango and papaya are good bulky fruits to boost the yield. Apple could be used instead of pear, but don't use too much as the pickle will become mushy. Use this pickle within a period of 3 months.

INGREDIENTS

2¾ lb. fruit, e.g. mango, papaya, banana, pear, nectarine

6 oz. fresh dates

1¼ cups red wine vinegar

¼ cup lime juice (bottled or fresh)

1 cup brown sugar

4 slices fresh ginger

½ cup broken walnut pieces

1 tsp. salt

METHOD

Peel and slice the fruit and put into a large saucepan. Pit and quarter the dates and add to the saucepan with the remaining ingredients. Simmer gently for 30 minutes.

Remove the ginger slices and pot while still hot.

TROPICAL JAM

Makes approximately 4 lb.

INGREDIENTS

2 lb. tart apples

juice and shells of 4 limes

2 mangoes, peeled, pitted and chopped

3 lb. sugar

6 passion fruit

METHOD

Peel, core and slice the apples into a large saucepan. Tie all the peel and trimmings in a piece of cheesecloth with the lime shells and mango trimmings. Place these in the saucepan. Add the lime juice and 5 cups water. Bring to a boil, cover and simmer for 1 hour.

Remove the bag of trimmings, squeezing out all the juice. Add the sugar, chopped mango, and sieved passion fruit to the pan. Heat gently, stirring, until the sugar dissolves. Bring to a hard boil and cook until setting point is reached (see Red Currant and Orange Jelly, page 117). Pot, cover, and label in the usual way.

MANGO & GREEN TOMATO CHUTNEY

Makes approximately 4 lb.

INGREDIENTS

2 lb. mangoes, peeled and quartered

1½ lb. tart apples, peeled and chopped

1 cup chopped onions

1 lb. green tomatoes, chopped

⅔ cup raisins

juice of 1 large lemon

2½ cups vinegar

2 tbsp. salt

¼ tsp. cayenne pepper

¼ tsp. nutmeg

3 bay leaves

1½ tbsp. lime juice

2 lb. brown sugar

METHOD

Place all the ingredients except the lime juice and sugar in a large bowl, mix thoroughly and leave to stand for at least 3 hours.

Transfer to a preserving pan, bring to a boil and simmer gently until tender, stirring frequently. Add the lime juice and sugar and stir until the sugar is dissolved. Continue to simmer until thick and of the desired consistency. Pour into warmed jars, cover, and label.

GOOSEBERRY & GARLIC CHUTNEY

Makes approximately 4½ lb.

INGREDIENTS

3 lb. gooseberries

2 cups chopped onions

½ lb. tart apples, chopped

8 cloves of garlic, crushed

2 tsp. salt

1 lb. sugar

1 tsp. chili powder

2½ cups vinegar

2 tbsp. oil

½ tsp. fenugreek seeds

METHOD

Trim the gooseberries and place in a large saucepan with the onions, apples, garlic, salt, sugar, chili powder, and vinegar.

Bring to a boil, reduce the heat and simmer for about 1 hour, stirring occasionally, until the fruit is pulpy and the chutney has thickened.

Heat the oil in a small pan, remove from the heat and add the fenugreek seeds. Leave for 2–3 minutes before stirring into the chutney with the oil.

Pot in warmed jars to mature for 3–4 weeks.

MANGO CHUTNEY

Makes approximately 4 lb.

This is the traditional chutney to serve with curried food. If green mangoes are unavailable, use firm plums to make a mock mango chutney.

INGREDIENTS

3 lb. green mangoes, peeled, halved, and pitted

4–6 tbsp. salt

4½ pt water

1 lb. sugar

2½ cups white wine vinegar

2 inch piece fresh root ginger, peeled and finely chopped

6 garlic cloves, crushed

2 tsp. hot chili powder

1 cinnamon stick

⅔ cup raisins

⅔ cup fresh dates, pitted and chopped

METHOD

Cut the mangoes into small pieces. Place in a mixing bowl and add the salt and water. Cover and set aside for 24 hours.

Place the sugar and vinegar in a large pan and bring to a boil. Add the drained mangoes and the remaining ingredients. Bring back to a boil, stirring occasionally.

Cook gently, uncovered, for about 1¼ hours until the chutney is thick. Discard the cinnamon stick. Ladle into warm jars, label, and store.

QUALITY PRODUCE

HOT LIME PICKLE

Makes approximately 1 lb.

INGREDIENTS

6 limes

2 tbsp. salt

2 tsp. finely chopped chili peppers

1 tbsp. roasted ground cumin

2 onions, chopped

⅔ cup oil

1¼ cups garlic vinegar

METHOD

Chop the limes and place in a large bowl. Mix the salt, chilies and cumin and stir into the limes. Cover and leave to marinate overnight.

Place the onion into a saucepan with the oil and cook until soft, without browning. Stir in the marinated limes and seasoning and cook, stirring continuously, for about 15 minutes. Add the vinegar, bring to a boil, reduce the heat and simmer for about 1 hour.

Spoon the pickle into warmed jars with the liquid, making sure that the fruit is fully covered. Cover immediately and allow to mature for 2 weeks before using.

Note: To roast cumin, place some cumin seeds in a small pan and heat gently until they change color. Allow to cool before grinding.

PINEAPPLE PICKLE

Makes approximately 2½ cups

INGREDIENTS

1 tsp. chili powder

1 tbsp. mustard seed

2 cloves garlic, crushed

1 tsp. grated fresh root ginger

⅓ cup oil

1 dried red chili

2 tbsp. soft brown sugar

½ tsp. salt

⅞ cup light malt vinegar

1 pineapple, peeled and finely chopped

METHOD

Place the chili powder, mustard seed, garlic, and ginger in a bowl and grind together.

Heat the oil in a saucepan, add the dried red chili and cook for 1–2 seconds. Stir in the ground spices, sugar, salt, and vinegar. Bring to a boil and cook for 2 minutes. Stir in the pineapple and cook for 10 minutes. Pack into an airtight jar and use within 1 month.

PAPAYA & ORANGE PICKLE
Makes approximately 2 lb.

INGREDIENTS

2 cups chopped onions

3 small cloves garlic, crushed

1 cup cider vinegar

1½ inch fresh root ginger, sliced

2 medium-sized papayas (approx 1½ lb.)

peeled peel and juice of 1 orange

6 cloves

3 dried red chilies

6 allspice berries

½ tsp. salt

½ cup light soft brown sugar

⅓ cup seeded raisins, chopped

METHOD

Place the onions, garlic, cider vinegar, and ginger in a saucepan and cook for 10 minutes to just soften the onion.

Halve the papayas, scoop out the seeds and peel. Cut the flesh into ½ inch dice, and add with the remaining ingredients to the pan.

Cook for about 15 minutes until the papaya is just cooked and still retains its shape. Remove the orange peel and whole spices, if liked. Remove the ginger and chilies unless a hot pickle is preferred. Pot into jars while still hot.

PLUM & PUMPKIN PICKLE

Makes approximately 5¼ lb.

This is a sweet and sour pickle ideal for pork and cheese. The pumpkin and onion should be slightly crisp.

INGREDIENTS

2 lb. piece of pumpkin

1 lb. onions, sliced

1¼ cups cider vinegar

6 cloves garlic, crushed

2 lb. plums, halved and pitted

3 bay leaves

½ oz. salt

⅔ cup golden raisins

1 tbsp. mustard seed

METHOD

Cut the flesh from the skin of the pumpkin and dice. Place in a large saucepan with the onions, cider vinegar, and garlic. Cook slowly to just soften the pumpkin so it remains a bit crisp – about 20 minutes.

Add the plums and bay leaves. Cook for a further 10–15 minutes to soften the plums without losing their shape. Stir in the remaining ingredients. Place in a large bowl, cover and leave for 1 week for the flavors to develop and the mustard seeds to swell. Stir from time to time.

Remove the bay leaves and pot in jars.

RED CURRANT & APPLE PICKLE

Makes approximately 2 lb.

INGREDIENTS

2 lb. red currants

1 lb. onions, chopped

1 lb. tart apples, peeled and diced

4 cloves garlic, crushed

1 oz. fresh root ginger

1 tsp. turmeric

1 tsp. salt

1 tsp. ground coriander

1⅓ cups brown sugar

1¼ cups white wine vinegar

METHOD

String the red currants and place in a large saucepan with the onions, apples, garlic, ginger, and remaining ingredients. Bring to a boil, lower the heat and simmer for about 1½ hours until reduced and thick.

Put into warmed pots and cover immediately. Allow to mature for 2 weeks before using.

SWEET PLUM CHUTNEY

Makes approximately 5½ lb.

INGREDIENTS

2½ lb. plums

1 lb. tart apples

1 cup onions

1⅓ cups pitted dates, chopped

⅔ cup golden raisins

juice of 1 lemon

1½ tbsp. salt

¼ tsp. ground nutmeg

1 tsp. crushed chilies

3 bay leaves

2½ cups malt vinegar

2 lb. brown sugar

1 tbsp. lime juice

METHOD

Wash, halve and pit the plums. Peel, core and finely chop the apples. Peel and finely chop the onion. Place the prepared fruits and onion in a large bowl with the chopped dates, golden raisins, lemon juice, salt, ground nutmeg, crushed chilies, and bay leaves. Stir in the vinegar, cover and leave for 3 hours. Transfer to a preserving pan, bring to a boil and simmer gently for about 45 minutes until the fruits are tender, stirring occasionally.

Stir in the sugar and lime juice. Bring back to a boil and simmer, stirring frequently, until the chutney is quite thick, about 15 minutes. Remove bay leaves.

Pour into clean, warm jars and cover with thin plastic and screwtop lids. Label and leave to become cold before storing for at least 3 months to mature.

QUINCE JELLY

Makes approximately 6½ lb.

Serve with cold meats, hot roast pork, game, or lamb.

INGREDIENTS

4 lb. quinces

7 pt water

3 lb. sugar

METHOD

Wash and chop the quinces and place in a large saucepan with 5 pt water. Cover and simmer gently until the fruit is soft – about 1 hour, depending on the ripeness of the fruit. When soft, squeeze the fruit with a potato masher.

Remove the pan from the heat, ladle the fruit into a jelly bag and allow to drip for 30 minutes. Return the pulp to the pan with the remaining water and simmer for a further 30 minutes. Ladle the fruit again into the jelly bag and leave to drip for several hours.

Measure the juice – it should yield about 7½ cups. Allow 1 lb. sugar to each 2½ cups juice. Bring the juice to a boil, add the sugar and stir over a low heat to dissolve the sugar. Bring to a boil and continue boiling until setting point is reached – about 10 minutes (the temperature should be 220°).

Remove any scum and pot quickly into warm, clean jars. Cover and label as before.

SPICED PICKLED PEARS

Makes 4 lb.

INGREDIENTS

3¼ lb. pears

1 tsp. mixed spice

1 tsp. ground nutmeg

1 tsp. ground cinnamon

1 lb. brown sugar

2½ cups malt vinegar

METHOD

Peel, halve and core the pears. Mix the spices with a little of the sugar and vinegar. Put the remaining sugar and vinegar in a large saucepan or preserving pan and add the blended spices.

Bring slowly to a boil, making sure the sugar is dissolved before it reaches boiling point. Put in the prepared pears and simmer until just tender.

Pack suitable warmed jars with pears. Reboil the syrup for 5–10 minutes and pour on to the pears, allowing the syrup to just flow over the rim of the jar. Cover quickly.

DAMSON CHEESE

Makes approximately 2–3 lb.

INGREDIENTS

3 lb. damsons

¾ cup water

1½ cups sugar to 1 lb. pulp

METHOD

Wash the damsons and remove any stems. Place in a large saucepan with the water, cover and simmer until really soft. Push through a nylon sieve, using a wooden spoon, and discard the pits.

Weigh the pulp and return to the saucepan with the required amount of sugar. Heat gently, stirring, until the sugar is dissolved.

Bring to a boil and boil gently, stirring continuously, until thick.

Pot in small jars, covering with a wax disc. Cover, label and date before storing.

Note: For a Spiced Damson Cheese to serve with meats, add 1 tsp. allspice.

SEVILLE ORANGE MARMALADE

Makes approximately 7 lb.

INGREDIENTS

3 lb. Seville oranges

12½ cups water

juice from 2 lemons

5 lb. sugar

METHOD

Scrub the oranges and place in large saucepan with the water. Bring to a boil, cover and reduce the heat. Simmer for 2–2¼ hours until the oranges are soft. Remove the fruit with a slotted spoon, reserving the liquid in the saucepan. Allow the oranges to cool.

Cut the oranges in half, remove the seeds and slice the flesh as thinly as possible. Return the oranges to the saucepan. Add the sugar and juice and heat gently, stirring, until the sugar is completely dissolved.

Bring to a boil and boil hard until setting point is reached (see Red Currant and Orange Jelly below).

Remove any scum and allow the marmalade to stand for 15 minutes before pouring into clean, warmed jars. Cover, label, and date.

RED CURRANT & ORANGE JELLY

Makes approximately 1½ lb.

INGREDIENTS

4 lb. red currants

4 medium-sized oranges

1 lb. sugar per 2½ cups juice

METHOD

Wash the red currants, leaving the stems on, and place in a preserving pan. Thinly peel the oranges and squeeze out the juice. Add the peel and the juice to the red currants. Simmer the fruit gently to soften – about 20 minutes.

Set up a jelly bag, carefully pour in the red currants and leave to strain until the fruit has cooled and is no longer dripping. Do not squeeze the jelly bag otherwise the jelly will become cloudy.

Measure the juice and pour into a preserving pan. Add required amount of sugar. Heat gently until the sugar has dissolved and bring to boiling point. Boil hard until setting point has been reached.

Test for set by pouring a teaspoon of jelly onto a cold saucer. Allow to cool. When pushed with a finger, the surface should crinkle. Alternatively, check with a candy thermometer that the jelly has reached 220°.

Quickly remove any scum and pour the jelly into warmed jars. Cover with waxed discs and cover, label, and date before storing.

117

STRAWBERRY & GOOSEBERRY JAM

Makes approximately 5 lb.

INGREDIENTS

1½ lb. gooseberries

⅔ cup water

1½ lb. strawberries, hulled

3 lb. sugar

METHOD

Wash and trim the gooseberries and place in a preserving pan with the water. Cook gently until they begin to soften. Add the strawberries and continue cooking until the fruit is soft. Remove the pan from the heat and stir in the sugar until dissolved.

Return the pan to the heat. Bring to a boil, stirring to make sure the sugar has completely dissolved, and cook rapidly until setting point is reached (see Red Currant and Orange Jelly above).

Allow the jam to stand for 5 minutes. Pour into warmed jars, cover, label, and date.

GLOSSARY OF FRUITS

APPLES, PEARS, AND QUINCES

APPLES – DESSERT

Eating apples are smaller than tart apples and sweeter in flavor. Some varieties cook better than others. Harvesting of apples takes place at different times of the year as eating apples do not store very well. However, apples are grown all over the world and are readily available all year. When cooked, they retain their shape longer than do cooking apples. **Use:** Fruit and savory salads and some traditional flans, tarts and pies, soups, fritters, and stuffings.

Most have a fairly bland flavor which makes them ideal for mixing with other fruits for color and texture. **Use:** Eat raw, poach in syrup or liqueurs, add to sweet and savory dishes, salads, appetizers with cheese. They can be fried as an accompaniment to pork or cooked whole with a roast. Add to pickles and chutneys.

QUINCES

Elongated, pear-shaped fruit with a downy green-ishy-yellow skin. The core has lots of seeds and the fruit is only eaten cooked. **Use:** Jams, jellies, and as an accom-paniment to meat.

APPLES – TART

These are larger than eating apples and soften more quickly on cooking. Some varieties are sharper than others. **Use:** Sweet and savory dishes, pies, puddings, flans, cakes, preserves, jam and jelly making, pickles, and chutneys.

PEARS

There are many varieties of pear. Some lend them-selves more to eating and others are only suitable for cooking because the texture is more granular.

FRUIT WITH PITS

APRICOTS

Apricots are in season in the summer months. They are also imported from various parts of the world. They are a most versatile fruit. **Use:** Sweet and savory dishes, pies, puddings, ice creams, sherbets, mousses, fruit purées, stuffings, gâteaux and cheesecakes, jams, preserves, chutneys, and pickles.

118

PEACHES

Fresh peaches are tender and juicy when ripe. There are two varieties, one with an orange-yellow flesh and one with white flesh which is more fragrant. **Use:** Peel and eat fresh. Use in jams, compôtes, flan fillings, fruit salads and desserts, or for garnishing meats and other savory dishes; preserve in syrup or liqueurs and use in chutneys.

DAMSONS

A small plum-like fruit, cultivated from a wild plum. Has quite a sharp, tangy flavor and mixes well with apple. **Use:** Jams, pies, pickles, chutneys. If puréed, it can be used in fruit fools, mousses, and soufflés.

NECTARINES

Similar to a peach, with a smoother skin. They have a juicy orange flesh. **Use:** Eaten raw or served with ham or pork, used in fruit salads, compôtes, flans and cheesecakes, preserved in syrup or liqueurs, made into jams and chutneys.

PLUMS

A very versatile fruit, with many varieties, available all year round.

They have sweet, fragrant flesh with a large pit in the center. **Use:** Eat raw or to make soups, soufflés and mousses, flans, tarts, pies, savory sauces, jams, jellies, juices, chutneys, and pickles. Use in cakes and baked puddings.

BERRIES, CHERRIES, AND GRAPES

BLACKBERRIES

These fruits are available from May to September and can be wild or cultivated. They are a most versatile fruit

which freezes well. **Use:** Preserves, tarts, pies, flans and summer puddings; they can be mixed with exotic fruits to make compôtes, wine, catsups, jams and relishes, and are ideal to mix with other fruits such as apples.

BLACK CURRANTS

These are a very rich fruit with a wonderful flavor and full of vitamin C.

They are often mixed with other fruits, such as apples and rhubarb. Black currants freeze well and can be bought frozen. **Use:** Pies, puddings, drinks, ice creams, fools, mousses, jams, fruit butters, and savory sauces to accompany rich meats.

CHERRIES

Sweet cherries are most readily available. There are a number of varieties but the most common are dark red. When bought, they should be eaten straight away as they do not keep long. Sour red cherries are available and are cooked in pies, pud-dings, and preserves. Frozen pitted cherries are readily available. **Use:** Pies, fruit salads, compôtes, sweet soups. They are also made into sauces to accompany rich meats such as duck and pork.

GRAPES

A vast number of grape varieties exist, white, black and red, with seeds and seedless. Some varieties are grown for winemaking. **Use:** The skins are edible and the fruit is mainly eaten raw, but they can be used in stuffings and in savory sauces to accompany chicken, pheasant, duck and other game birds, and in savory and fruit salads.

STRAWBERRIES

Strawberries are "false" fruit, the actual fruit being the seeds on the outside. There are many varieties, some of which freeze better than others, but a purée freezes the best. Wild strawberries have a different flavor; they are not easily available but are well worth growing if you have the space. **Use:** Eat on their own with cream and sugar. Make into jams, jellies, fruit fillings and toppings, fruit and savory salads, mousses, creams, soufflés, drinks, pancake fillings, and garnishes. Strawberry shortcake is popular.

TAYBERRIES

A cross between a blackberry and a raspberry, developed in Scotland. When ripe, a large juicy red to purple berry, with a delicious flavor. The small core could be off-putting to some. **Use:** Eat raw, mash and purée for fillings, pies, flans, sherbets, ice creams, cheesecakes, jams, and jellies.

LOGANBERRIES

Large, elongated fruit, purple-red in color, similar to a blackberry. The juicy flesh goes mushy very quickly. **Use:** Pies, puddings, flans, tarts, jams, puréed for ice creams, sherbets, mousses, soufflés, and sauces.

CAPE GOOSEBERRIES/PHYSALIS

These look like small Oriental lanterns with a papery, yellowish covering. When this is removed a small yellow fruit about the size of a cherry is revealed. **Use:** Eaten raw, added to fruit salads, coated in fondant, chocolate or glacé icing, and used as petits fours.

WHORTLEBERRIES

There are two varieties, a blue oval berry, and a red one. **Use:** Ideal for jams, jellies, and juices.

MULBERRIES

There are three types of mulberry, white, black, and red. They are elongated, bramble-type fruits, with a sharp, tangy, sweet flavor. **Use:** Eaten fresh, used in fruit salads, flan fillings, jams, and jellies.

RASPBERRIES

A popular soft fruit which freezes well. Sweet, with a characteristic aroma, it is grown all over the world. **Use:** Eat with sugar and cream, make into jams, jellies, vinegar, milkshakes, ice cream, sherbets, mousses, soufflés, summer pudding, sauces.

BLUEBERRIES

A fairly large fruit with a colorless juice, often confused with bilberries which have a purple juice. They have a delicate, slightly scented flavor, and may be eaten fresh with cream. **Use:** Poached, making a good topping for cheesecakes and fillings for sponge flans, soups, muffins, pies, filling for pancakes, and stirred into fromage frais.

RED CURRANTS

Translucent, usually bright red berries, but there is also a white variety which is sweeter. **Use:** Fresh in fruit salads and desserts, or made into jams, jellies, or sauces.

CRANBERRIES

Cranberries have a good flavor and color and are very tangy. They combine well with other fruits. **Use:** Traditionally served as a sauce with turkey; made into relishes, used in stuffings, spiced sauces, and drinks. They are also used as an ingredient in meat pies and pâtés.

GOOSEBERRIES

A plump, slightly hairy green or red fruit. When in season they are plentiful and they are easy to grow. When ripe, they can be eaten raw. **Use:** A good fruit for cooking, making purées for fools, mousses, soufflés, jams, pickles, chutneys, pies, and puddings. Can be used in stuffings and sauces.

CITIRUS

CLEMENTINES

A variety of mandarin orange, generally seedless. **Use:** Eaten raw, added to fruit salads, caramelized and preserved whole in syrups, sweet or spiced.

MANDARINS

Small, round citrus fruit, frequently crossed with other citrus varieties. **Use:** Peeled and eaten fresh, used in ice creams, fruit salads, jams and marmalades, bottled in syrups, and used as a garnish.

LIMES

Small, green citrus fruit used in the same way as oranges and lemons. The flesh is bright green and more acid and fragrant than that of a lemon. **Use:** Lemonade, juices, jams, pickles, sherbets, jellies, and garnishes.

GRAPEFRUIT

There are two varieties of grapefruit, one with pale yellow segments and the other pink to blood red. The redder the color, the sweeter the taste. Some varieties have seeds and some do not. They are available throughout the year. **Use:** Peeled and eaten in segments like an orange, or halved and the flesh scooped out to serve as an appetizer, plain or broiled with sugar. Segments can be added to fruit salads, sherbets and sauces. They are also used for making marmalade and squeezed as a juice to drink.

LEMONS

An important part of a large citrus family. They are available all the year round. Some varieties are better than others because of the thickness of skin. Those with thinner skins are better. **Use:** In sweet and savory dishes, marmalades, sherbets, ice creams, mousses, jams, jellies, and drinks. The peel can be candied and used in cakes. The juice is often used to bring out the flavor of a recipe.

MINNEOLA

Another member of the citrus family, a cross between a tangerine and a grapefruit. The flesh is sweet and very juicy with a tangy fragrance. **Use:** As versatile as other citrus fruits.

TEMPLES

Another citrus fruit, a hybrid, called the "King Orange". Juicy and tangy, containing large seeds. **Use:** As for other citrus fruits.

SATSUMAS

A member of the citrus family. A sharp, small tangerine-type fruit, with few, if any, seeds. **Use:** Peel and eat raw, add to winter fruit salads and savory salads. The rind may be used to flavor preserves. The fruit can be scooped from the skins, made into sherbet and returned to the shell and frozen. May be preserved whole in syrups or liqueurs.

ORANGES

There are many varieties available all year round. Seville oranges are for marmalade making or any recipe where a bitter orange flavor would be needed. **Use:** Mainly eaten raw, but they are very versatile, their strong flavor is used in both sweet and savory dishes. They are often used with chocolate, as the flavors complement each other well.

122

ORTANIQUES

Another citrus fruit, a blend of orange and tangerine. They are large, with orange-yellow flesh, sweet and very juicy. **Use:** Eat fresh. Squeeze for drinks and use in fruit salads.

TANGERINES

Part of the citrus family. They are very juicy and usually have pips. **Use:** Eat fresh, add to fruit salads, sherbets, ice creams and granitas, caramelized, use whole in syrups, marmalade, jellies, and garnishes. Can be served with chicken.

UGLIS

A cross between a tangerine, orange, and grapefruit. A misshapen fruit with a knobbly skin, a mixture of orange and green in color. The fruit is delicious, pinkish yellow, and sweeter than grapefruit. **Use:** The same as oranges and grapefruit – salads, desserts, marmalades, and the peel can be candied. Dressings for salads.

POMELOS

A member of the citrus family, similar to a grapefruit. **Use:** Eat fresh, sprinkled with sugar. Make into jams or jellies, or add to fruit salads.

EXOTIC

CARAMBOLAS

Also known as star fruit because of the shape of the slices. The fruit has a slightly crisp texture and a very delicate flavor which can be quite sharp. **Use:** In fruit salads, glazed on top of cheesecakes, flans, and gâteaux.

MANGOSTEENS

These have a dark red-purple skin which is quite tough and great care needs to be taken when cutting through this skin to get to the fruit as the knife easily slips off. Use a knife with a serrated edge. The fruit is waxy-white in color and quite sweet and fragrant to eat. Some segments may contain quite a large seed. **Use:** Peel and eat raw, add to fruit salads. Sieve the juice to make a sherbet.

CUSTARD APPLES

A green fruit, with a thick crusty skin which, when ripe, starts to split. The creamy white flesh is sweet and juicy, quite fibrous, and contains many inedible seeds. **Use:** Eaten raw. Can be sieved and the juice used in fruit salads.

DATES

Fresh, ripe dates are eaten on their own. They do not keep very long but are very versatile. **Use:** Can be made into spreads by mixing with cream cheese and chopped apple, used in cakes and fruit salads and added to chutneys and pickles. At Christmas time they are stuffed with marzipan.

GUAVAS

There are two varieties of guava, one an oval fruit slightly larger than a pear, with a creamy-colored skin, and the other a rounder green fruit which comes from Thailand, Malaysia and Indonesia. **Use:** The seeds are scooped out and the flesh is eaten alone or used in fruit salads. They can be poached in a sugar syrup. (See recipe for Guava and Turkey Kebabs on page 41.)

DURIAN

A large green fruit, covered in spikes, which has a lingering, unpleasant odor. Has to be cracked open carefully to expose segments of sweet, smooth-textured flesh. **Use:** Boil unripe fruit and use in soups and vegetable dishes. It can be incorporated into ice cream.

MANGOES

These are grown in many countries, giving a variety of sizes. They are oval, thick-skinned fruit which have a deep red blush when fully ripe. The peach-colored flesh has a pleasant tang when firm and is very sweet when soft and fully ripened. **Use:** The flesh can be eaten fresh, sprinkled with lemon or orange juice. An ideal way of serving, which complements both flavors, is with sliced papaya. They are also used in chutneys, pickles, fruit salads, hors d'oeuvres, ice creams, sherbets, and mousses.

RAMBUTANS

A member of the lychee family, it has reddish skin with untidy, soft spines or hairs. The flesh is pale yellow and translucent, sweet and pleasantly scented, but not as flavorsome as that of the lychee. **Use:** Eat fresh, or use in fruit salads.

PERSIMMONS

There are two types of persimmon: one is a pale orange, round fruit with flesh the same color and large pips; the other, which is called sharon fruit, has been developed in Israel and has no pips or core. **Use:** Eat raw, slice into salads and use for sauces.

LYCHEES

Small, cherry-sized fruit with a knobbly red or brown skin and sweet, translucent flesh with a distinctive perfumed taste. **Use:** Peeled and eaten raw or added to fruit salads, sherbets, and sauces; cooked with pork and chicken dishes.

PAPAYAS

Also known as paw-paws, they are greenish-yellow long fruit with orange flesh and lots of seeds which need to be scooped out. They are sweet in flavor. **Use:** They complement mangoes and are ideal in exotic fruit salads, or as an appetizer with strawberries. They can be served as a vegetable and the juice can be used as a meat tenderizer.

PASSION FRUIT

A round fruit, purple in color, with a thin tough skin, which crinkles when ripe. They must feel heavy, as moisture is lost from the fruit quickly. The juicy green flesh has soft edible seeds. Granadilla is a yellow fruit similar to passion fruit and is used in the same way. **Use:** Scoop out the flesh and mix with whipped or sour cream or fromage frais. Use for fruit salads, decorating pavlovas, and jams.

CHINESE GOOSEBERRIES

These are brown, slightly hairy fruits, with a thin skin covering a tender green flesh with a ring of fine, dark seeds in the middle. The sweet sour taste is delicate and refreshing. Chinese gooseberries have become a modern much-used fruit. **Use:** In salads, both sweet and savory, cheesecakes, garnishes, sherbets, mousses, starters, pavlovas, chutneys, and relishes.

KUMQUATS

Kumquats are thumb-sized oval oranges with an edible skin, sometimes with many seeds. The whole fruit should be eaten as the skin and flesh complement each other and they are too small to be segmented. When using for cooking it is best to halve them and remove the seeds. **Use:** Savory dishes, sauces, fruit salads, marmalade, and bottled in syrup or brandy. The fruit may be pricked and left to flavor vodka and white rum, or any other alcohol.

LUNGANS

Similar to a lychee, with a smooth skin. Fleshy, sweetly scented fruit inside with a large pip. **Use:** Peeled and eaten raw, or added to fruit salads.

FIGS

Dark purple-skinned figs are most readily available. They have bright red centers packed with tiny seeds. The flavor is sweet and aromatic but sometimes insipid. The skin is edible. **Use:** Eaten raw, sliced and served with ham, salami or cheese, sprinkled with liqueur and used as part of a compote, made into fig soufflé, mousses, or served with cream.

MEDLARS

Rust-brown in color with hard, rough skin. The fruit contains five small pits and not much flesh. The flavor is slightly spiced and rather tart. Loquats are a Japanese medlar and are a pale yellow to deep orange in color. The flavor of these is a mixture of apple and apricot. **Use:** Should be cooked and sieved before making into jams, jellies, or purées. Loquats can be eaten fresh or made into jams, compôtes, or fruit salads.

PINEAPPLES

A very familiar, versatile fruit, very juicy when ripe. **Use:** Eat raw with liqueur sprinkled over, use in fruit salads, flans, hot puddings, cakes, meat and fish dishes, salads, jams, pickles, and drinks.

POMEGRANATES

A round, hard fruit with a leathery yellow-red skin. It is full of edible seeds embedded in juicy dark red flesh. **Use:** Eat raw with the flesh scooped out, or serve in fruit salads.

PRICKLY PEARS

The fruit of a cactus plant. Orange to bright red when ripe, with prickly spines. A watery fruit with lots of edible seeds. Rub the fruit to get rid of spines, cut in half and scoop out the flesh. **Use:** Eat raw, or use in fruit salads.

TAMARILLOS

A tree tomato, an oval fruit with a thin skin. Ripens to an orange/yellow color or red, the yellow type tending to be sweeter in flavor. The flesh is firm with a pulpy center, which is sweet and full of flavor. They are thought to  resemble Cape gooseberries in taste. They blend very well with Chinese gooseberries. **Use:** Can be eaten raw, but needs to be sweetened. Otherwise, stewed, baked, or broiled. Can be made into jam.

BANANAS

There are three varieties of banana available: the large, familiar, yellow ones which are eaten raw, the miniature ones known as apple bananas, suitable for eating and cooking, and the green bananas known as plantains. Unless they are to be eaten immediately after peeling, they need to be tossed in lemon juice to stop discoloration.

Do not keep bananas in a refrigerator. If they are stored with other fruit they will cause these to ripen more quickly. If you require a hard avocado to ripen quickly, put it in a bag with a ripe banana and leave it in a warm place for 24 hours. **Use:** A very versatile fruit for both sweet and savory dishes: cheesecakes, chiffon pies, brûlées, ice cream, drinks and as an accompaniment to barbecued food. Bananas go very well with bacon, as an accompaniment to chicken.

MELONS

There are various types of melon, the flesh of some being orange. The watermelon is different in texture and appearance. **Use:** Mostly eaten raw as appetizers with ginger and sugar, otherwise added to salads, served with shellfish, ham and cold meats, or made into sherbets, and ice creams.

RHUBARB

A stem grown from a crown in the ground. It is very versatile and mixes well with other fruits and spices. **Use:** Rhubarb can only be used cooked. Stewed and served with cream or custard, used in pastry pies, hot puddings, fools, mousses, souffles, compôtes, flans and tarts, jams, sauces, pickles, and chutneys.

INDEX

126